Robyn Lea is an acclaimed photographer, writer and director whose work has been published in *Elle Decor*, *The New York Times*, *Vogue* and *Architectural Digest*. She is the author of *Dinner with Jackson Pollock* and *Dinner with Georgia O'Keeffe*. Her work has also featured in more than ten solo exhibitions around the world.

BOHEMIAN LIVING

Creative Homes Around the World

ROBYN LEA

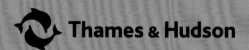

Thames & Hudson

CONTENTS

INTRODUCTION

I often feel as though my camera is a magic key. A key to adventure, a key to connecting with people and learning about the human spirit, and a key to entering the private worlds of others – worlds that would have otherwise been inaccessible. This key also sometimes requires me to take small risks: to stay with people I have never met, ask personal questions, and travel to remote places – often on my own. Entering the homes of the artists and creators in this book, I have come to understand that for many of them, their unique personal spaces are essential to their internal dialogue, and sometimes even central to their emotional wellbeing.

Along the way, I drove thousands of kilometres across the USA and Australia, and took trains and planes across Europe, often listening to the recordings of my interviews and losing myself in the remarkable stories that these artists and collectors shared with me. Each of the twenty homes and creative spaces featured in these pages are imbued with these stories – sometimes joyous, sometimes devastating, but always authentic and ultimately uplifting. Included in the mix is a vast studio in downtown New York, a light-filled apartment overlooking the ancient canals of Milan's art and design district, a treehouse on stilts in the woods north of New Orleans and an apartment in Paris that has been converted into the most secret of private museums.

The homes of these modern-day bohemians break almost every traditional interior decorating rule. Why not put muted pink paint in the same room as a bright capsicum-green? Why strive to make a room feel bigger if an avalanche of objects and furniture feeds your work and your sense of self? Why not get out a brush and paint shapes around a room, or take a knife and engrave 'I love you' into the wall of the studio you share with your partner? And why is it wrong to live our grown-up lives with as much of the freedom and sparkle of childhood as we can? Whether consciously or not, the subjects in this book are not imprisoned by others' expectations. And it's liberating.

Several of the artists have chosen itinerant lives, while others practise communal living with people of the same beliefs and values, centred around a collective approach to the sharing of resources and a rejection of consumerism and patriarchal structures. One of the artists shares her home with her ex-husband and their child, with new lovers openly accepted into the mix. Another replicates the best of her childhood, which fused communal living with the hippy and drag culture of 1970s San Francisco. In yet another configuration, a long-term couple live in neighbouring apartments, so they can each have their own space whenever they need it.

When I began this project in early 2017, I thought it would be a book about artistic and unconventional homes around the world. However, deeper themes began to emerge early in the project. Many of the interiors were much more than simply attractive to the people who created them. They were an important creative expression. Some of the subjects felt they could not grow, thrive or survive in environments that felt alien to them. In Bordeaux, paper artist Claire Guiral explains, 'I think that if you placed me in a white, very clean apartment with a lot of plastic, I would die very quickly.' In Milan, Barnaba Fornasetti also speaks decisively about why he cannot spend long periods away from home. 'I am absolutely addicted to it. My home is a protective oasis in perpetual transformation. It represents my life: my job, my interests and my philosophy – all entwined.' Visual artist and collector Greg Irvine says, 'This house is an extension of one of my paintings. Instead of painting with paint, I paint with objects. [It] is a succession of still lifes, which I change constantly.'

Art and creativity can be potent tools used to distil difficult emotional challenges. Painting the world bright, or creating a beautiful private universe, can help keep darkness at bay. 'I have a conscious awareness that I am fighting depression every single minute of my life … I have found my creative work is one of the best ways to harness it,' says one of the homeowners. While not all of their most sensitive stories are shared in these pages, their feelings radiate like colourful symbols of hope and triumph through many of these rooms. Like talismans, the spaces have a deeply positive impact on the lives of those who create them, and attract like-minded people to their realms. This in turn helps provide another of the greatest of human needs: community and a sense of belonging to one's tribe.

Like a map of the spirit transposed onto walls, doors and floors, each interior has a rich and complex personality. In choosing from and rejecting an infinite number of colours, textures, layers and forms, a language is established. It's like a fingerprint; unique to each creator. As a result, these spaces are impossible to replicate in any meaningful way, which makes them all the more appealing.

The relationship between self and space is both a pivotal theme in this book and an ongoing interest of many of the people featured. 'A space can either enhance or take away from your character. I can't relax in a sterile environment, or a careless environment. It makes me depressed. It makes me sad. I don't even feel like myself anymore,' Australian artist Luke Sciberras explains from his home in rural New South Wales. Almost 16,000 kilometres away in her New York apartment, Rebecca Purcell says, 'I look at this space and ask myself, "How does this express me specifically?" It is definitely all parts of me *outside* of myself. So my home's personality is my personality.'

For some, like Rebecca Rebouché in New Orleans, creating an interior is like a joyful performance, provoking a stimulating internal conversation. 'In your home, you get to be the playmaker. You have the marionettes, you're making them dance and

creating an environment that you can bounce off, and be in context with, and continuity with.' Gavin Brown explains his own exuberant approach to his apartment in St Kilda, Melbourne. 'I create the reality I want around me. People can say I live in a fantasy, but I think we all end up living in a bubble, so why not create a beautiful bubble?'

For most of the people in this book, home is an inspiring refuge that feeds their creative work and provides them with enormous comfort. Nomadic artist Francesco Clemente, however, intentionally leaves his home to travel whenever he begins to feel settled. He admits he is uncomfortable with comfort, and comfortable with discomfort. 'The strategy of my work is nomadic. What that means is that I spend my life trying to displace myself, displace my views, displace my point of view and find myself in between places. The fact that I have more than one place in different locales, in different countries, really has to do with the organisational side of that idea.'

One of the things they all have in common is a rejection of mass-produced objects and furniture in favour of idiosyncratic décor and unique pieces. Textile designer Peter Curnow's viewpoint is typical. 'I don't want a house that looks like it's just been pulled out of a catalogue. But good luck to whoever does want that! I have no interest in what is fashionable or what isn't. I just can't relate to that, and it has nothing to do with me.'

Several of the chapters in the book showcase homes that are in equal part art installation and living environment. On J Morgan Puett's property in Pennsylvania, for example, there is a tiny one-room cabin that is a replica of her late father's queen bee grafting hut. The original building was burnt down one night, along with all their beehives, by right-wing opponents of her father's political views. Years later, Morgan and her artist friends built a replica. They pasted pages from beekeepers' manuals to its interior walls and the custom-made wallpaper was gently coated in a thin film of beeswax. When the hut was completed, it assuaged the trauma of the fires that Morgan witnessed when she was a child.

Throughout these pages are many objects and items of furniture that represent the spirit and memories of loved ones. In Bella Meyer's living room in New York is a large desk where she likes to sit and work among her piles of books and papers. Decades ago, young Bella sat near her grandfather, the late artist Mark Chagall, as he worked at this same desk. Chagall talked to her about the importance of the simple things in life. His lessons, like his paintings and the handsome wooden desk, still resonate and inspire her today, almost half a century after his death.

Similarly, some of Robert Baines's most treasured possessions come from his late father's upholstery and French polishing workshop. His father taught him how to use each tool to prepare the furniture frames for new upholstery. Robert's father died when he was eight and the workshop was closed, although his spirit remains bound in his tools. Robert is now a goldsmith and he uses his father's tools in his art practice. He creates jewellery and small sculptures that, in the ultimate tribute to his late father, are collected by some of the most prestigious museums and galleries in the world.

Home is like a theatre for several of the artists featured in this book, a buoyant extension of their artistry. 'My home is my stage, my jewel box, my haven and my cabinet of curiosities. I get to edit my personal drama there,' says Gavin Brown.

A similar sentiment is held by Rebecca Rebouché. 'What we consider decoration is actually the creation of the set and the scene for your life and your character. The internal landscape is very rich, it's full of possibility and I think it needs a stage. That's what home is – a stage for the story that is happening inside you.'

For some, home is like a bigger version of the childhood bedrooms they cherished. For others, it is the home they wanted but didn't have. Peter Curnow's father wouldn't allow him to attach anything to his bedroom walls, and now virtually every available inch of wall space in his apartment is covered. Sydney-based artist Joshua Yeldham was removed from his family home when he was eight and sent to boarding school. He now keeps his own family close, enveloping them in strong wings like an owl in a large feathered nest. As a child, Nathalie Lété wanted to be surrounded by beautiful and colourful things. In her adult life,

she has created a home, studio and world of fabrics, ceramics, dolls, paintings and accessories that have sent joyous ripples around the world.

This is not a 'how to' book, nor is it a book with interiors you can easily replicate in your own home. Instead, it's a signed permission slip that allows you to trust every quirky idea that you have ever had, honour that intuitive voice when it bubbles to the surface, and explore the decorating dreams you had once dismissed as childish.

In a similar vein to the slow-food movement, this book celebrates the 'slow house', whose rooms are formed over a lifetime of collecting, creating and layering. It's a cure for image fatigue, and a reminder that status seeking and prestige purchases do not feed the soul. These interiors are created not to impress others, but as an expression of their owners' inner lives.

The path I followed while completing this book was full of surprises, diversions, new friendships and old connections. I realised that this was much more than an interiors book when I began to cry while interviewing several of my subjects, overwhelmed by the depth of emotion in their stories. Often, on long drives home across states and mountain ranges, I would reflect on my own life and my need for a home that nourishes and inspires. I did accept offers to stay overnight in the homes of people I had never met before, and I was surprised and moved when I quickly felt as if I was among family.

On further reflection, though, it made sense that I found so many kindred spirits, because this project began with a list. The list was based almost entirely on my personal response to each subject's artwork or creative interiors. Long before I arrived on their doorsteps, I felt like I was already in dialogue with their artwork, which spoke to me in a language of symbols, colour and form. What became clear as I worked on the project was that many people in these pages have created homes, studios and work that feed their desire to live. They have built a sense of place that is deeply entwined with their emotional needs, that provides an antidote to suffering, and is an inspiration to us all. – RL

REBECCA REBOUCHÉ

The Treehouse,
the Warehouse and the Little Loft

As Rebecca Rebouché rests her cheek on the bark of an ancient tree and wraps her arms around its 200-year-old trunk, it looks for a moment as if she has disappeared into one of her paintings. In her world, beds float on clouds, birds wear golden crowns, white swans ride on elephants' backs and giant white rabbits play the violin. She often paints trees and their branches sprout not just leaves, fruit and flowers, but musical instruments, bicycles and majestic sailing boats.

Rebecca is a contemporary folk artist who lives near the Mississippi River in the New Orleans neighbourhood known as the Bywater. Her one-bedroom loft is part of an apartment complex located in a converted 1920s sewing factory. The building houses an eclectic mix of writers, photographers, painters, performers and actors. It was established after Hurricane Katrina by the local government to provide subsidised housing for working artists. The loft provides Rebecca with 'a refuge that is kind of private. It's a little cabin, a sanctuary that is all mine – like a ship where I eat and sleep between other adventures.'

Rebecca has always lived close to water and she feels deeply connected to its rhythms and tides. Her conversation is peppered with water themes. She describes her living quarters as ships, and frequently depicts bodies of water in her work. *Beyond and Below* is a series of eighteen paintings that she created in 2017 'with celestial and aquatic imagery that depicts the furthest reaches of our human experience, beyond this world and this consciousness, below the surface, the soil, the ocean'. The painting *Night Swim* features a magnificent Siamese fighting fish living underground in a black pool of water filled with stars. In *How Whales Fly,* a whale is carried through the water by a flock of white birds,

while *Fathom* depicts a tree whose roots are held underwater by a ship's anchor.

Rebecca often paints *en plein air* by the banks of Lake Pontchartrain or the shores of nearby swamps, rivers and bayous. 'Water comes from the skies and the weather, so affects our moods. It's in our tears and it's in our bodies. I think it's a great metaphor, not only for impermanence, but for all of the things that we don't know – for the unconscious, for movement and fluidity.' She also finds meaning in its colour. 'There's something mesmerising about blue, the colour of sea and sky, below us and above us. It is the colour of heartbreak and expansiveness, night and day.'

Rebecca also uses water and nature themes to decorate her apartment, an activity that is another expression of her creative outlook. 'What we consider decoration is actually the creation of the set and the scene for your life and your character. The internal landscape is very rich, it's full of possibility and I think it needs a stage. That's what home is – a stage for the story that is happening inside you.' Sometimes she literally adorns a room from floor to ceiling with her work – designing the rugs, covering a sofa in a handmade quilt and decorating the walls with murals and paintings. 'You get to be the playmaker. You have the marionettes, you're making them dance and creating an environment that you can bounce off, and be in context with, and continuity with.'

The combined sitting and dining area in her apartment is framed on one side by a leather chesterfield sofa that she inherited from a film set, and on the other by a 1930s British campaign chest. She discovered the fall-front secretaire chest in a consignment store and the attraction was instant. 'This belongs to me – this is the missing piece.' Its little pigeon holes and recessed brass handles and trims reminded her of adventure stories, of travellers packing their possessions into steamer trunks for a long voyage by sea to a new home in a foreign land.

Once it was installed in her apartment, the chest was soon covered in an avalanche of paintings and elaborately decorated headpieces, creating an informal shrine to the annual New Orleans Mardi

Gras carnival. 'The headdresses and costumes I make are an extension of my artwork, and Mardi Gras day is when I get to embody the artwork. The metaphor of the human spirit triumphing over darkness is revealed to me as we parade through the streets adorned and dancing. I call it "The Beautiful Blur".'

Rebecca is a member of the Societé de Sainte Anne, a krewe known in New Orleans for their elaborate handmade Mardi Gras costumes. Their Mardi Gras rituals follow a similar pattern each year. 'We wake at sunrise on Fat Tuesday to the clanging of the Skull and Bones Gang who go out before dawn and parade through the streets to wake people up.' The krewe members meet to admire each other's costumes before parading through the streets of the Bywater, Faubourg Marigny and the French Quarter. Later, when they arrive on the banks of the Mississippi, the band plays the gospel tune 'Just a Closer Walk with Thee' as they sprinkle the ashes of lost loved ones into the river and support each other in collective mourning. 'Members carry colourful ribbon hoops that they dip into the river water and raise into the wind so that the water droplets casting off the ribbons baptise everyone standing on shore. It's a moving moment of silence amid all the revelry.'

On Bacchus Sunday, Rebecca joins in a parade called Box of Wine with a group called the Rosies, named after rosé wine. The Rosies carry boxes of cheap wine that they dispense into the mouths of the onlookers who line the street. 'It's a rowdy, fun time.' The Rosies choose their annual costume theme based on a type of wine. Sangria was a recent theme and Rebecca created an Andalusian feria-inspired headdress from silk flowers, feathers and costume jewellery attached to a leather base, which she wore with a floral dress, lace tights, and shoes she decorated with fabric, feathers and glitter.

Rebecca balances her love of costume, music, community and revelry with quiet reflection and time to herself. This dichotomy is mirrored in the decoration of the spaces she inhabits – her apartment, her studio and a house in the forest she calls her 'treehouse'. The rooms are either exuberantly covered with images, objects, text and collage, or are visually quiet and spare.

Bedrooms are decorated with special consideration. Sleep is a sacred state for Rebecca, 'like bathing in a forest of mysteries – and to wake is to be uprooted from the soil of slumber and only half-remember the journey. I had a lot of my artwork and visual stimuli in my bedroom and I felt it was overwhelming so I took everything off the wall and made this sanctuary – a blank space. I struggle with sleep, so now when it is time to go to bed, there is somewhere to rest where there is peace, and there isn't anything begging to be resolved or thought about.' She used a deep-charcoal matt paint on several of the bedroom walls to create a cave-like calming feel and hung a simple canopy of fine white muslin above the bed, which gives her a feeling of being inside a cocoon. 'When I don't have a canopy, it feels like there is too much space. Being in confined spaces is comforting. It is very natural to want to know exactly where "the edge" is.'

'There's something mesmerising about blue … It is the colour of heartbreak and expansiveness, night and day.'

In contrast to her compact apartment, Rebecca's studio is a vast cavernous space located in the industrial quarter of New Orleans, on the gritty working-class fringes of the city. The space allows her to work on large-scale commissions for a loyal clientele around the globe. She also creates extensive bodies of work for exhibitions from New York to Los Angeles. The studio is home to personal treasures, like a steamer trunk full of her private diaries, which provide an undercurrent of inspiration for her work.

Perhaps it is Rebecca's 'treehouse', located in the North Covington woods, where place and person feel most unified. The three-storey house is set on stilts among a forest of pine, oak and magnolia trees. Reeds surround a tiny pond to the left of the sandy driveway. A white grand piano sits in the forest, baby ferns grow underfoot and strings of tiny lights illuminate the trees at night. The large windows of the treehouse face north, creating the best light for painting. They also provide an observation area to watch for woodland animals, and many of these visitors feature in Rebecca's work.

Rebecca and her former partner began renting the house in 2010 and, for a time after their relationship ended, the property was a symbol of sadness and loss for Rebecca. 'It was like a ship I was sailing through the forest. It became a vessel for my solitude.' It slowly evolved as a place of two extremes: 'either me on my own, to think and work and be away' or a gathering place for dozens of musicians and artists at one of her famous forest parties. The first party she hosted there was a 'bluegrass pickin' party' inspired by traditional South Louisiana gatherings. Guests arrived with guitars, harmonicas, banjos and mandolins and played and sang together among the starlit trees. Each party since has had a different theme. In autumn and winter, friends gather around outdoor fires with blankets and sing songs by moonlight. In summer, they swim and sleep in the horse pasture under the midnight sky.

In 2014, Rebecca hosted a party centred around an exhibition of her work in the treehouse, *The Unlikely Naturalist Part 2: Modern Mythology.* Old friends and new flocked to the show and slept that night in the forest and nearby fields. Folk artist Dustan Louque imbued the atmosphere with what Rebecca describes as a 'sonic dreamscape love letter to Mother Earth'. Rebecca encourages her guests to be wild, free and unencumbered. 'You can make noise, you don't have to be quiet, you can sleep outside, you can climb a tree, you can literally just be loose or still, calm or loud, or whatever you need to be.'

These gatherings seem like a natural extension of the quilting community that Rebecca was born into. As a child, she would play underneath the quilting frame, listening to the women's stories and watching as they created decorative patterns from fabric saved from flour sacks. She now designs her own quilts and creates hand-appliquéd artworks.

Inherited family quilts cover her beds and couches, and quilts often feature in her paintings.

Rebecca often creates works in a series that might include over thirty paintings and several hand-stitched pieces. She describes her Fall 2010 series *Unearthed* as a 'journey from a remembered birth to an imagined death using all five senses'. Her emotionally charged spring 2010 series, *Lay Your Burden Down,* was a cathartic outpouring made 'while sharing a studio with twenty cats – broke and heartbroken'. In 2012, *The Unlikely Naturalist* was inspired by her travels through the American South and references southern Gothic literature by William Faulkner, Eudora Welty, Walker Percy and Tennessee Williams among others. Her ongoing series *My Red Balloon* was inspired by Albert Lamorisse's 1956 short film *Le Ballon Rouge*, in which a boy creates an imaginary friend from a balloon. Rebecca uses the balloon metaphor to explore themes of 'longing, friendship, love, loyalty and ultimately impermanence, loss, and the transformation of letting go'.

Rebecca is often asked why she doesn't relocate to a big urban centre like New York City, but her loyalty to New Orleans is strong. She loves the rhythm of life there, where nature and the Mississippi River dictate the mood, where it feels like there is endless time and space for dreaming, music and friends. One of her favourite pastimes involves cancelling all plans and heading to Fontainebleau State Park where she strings a hammock between two cypress trees by the shores of Lake Pontchartrain to read, paint, look to the sky or just float her thoughts away on a water view. As the tide rises, the base of each tree is covered with water, making gentle swirling patterns. The scene looks a lot like a possible subject for a new painting. ◆

> She loves the rhythm of life [in New Orleans], where nature and the Mississippi River dictate the mood …

15

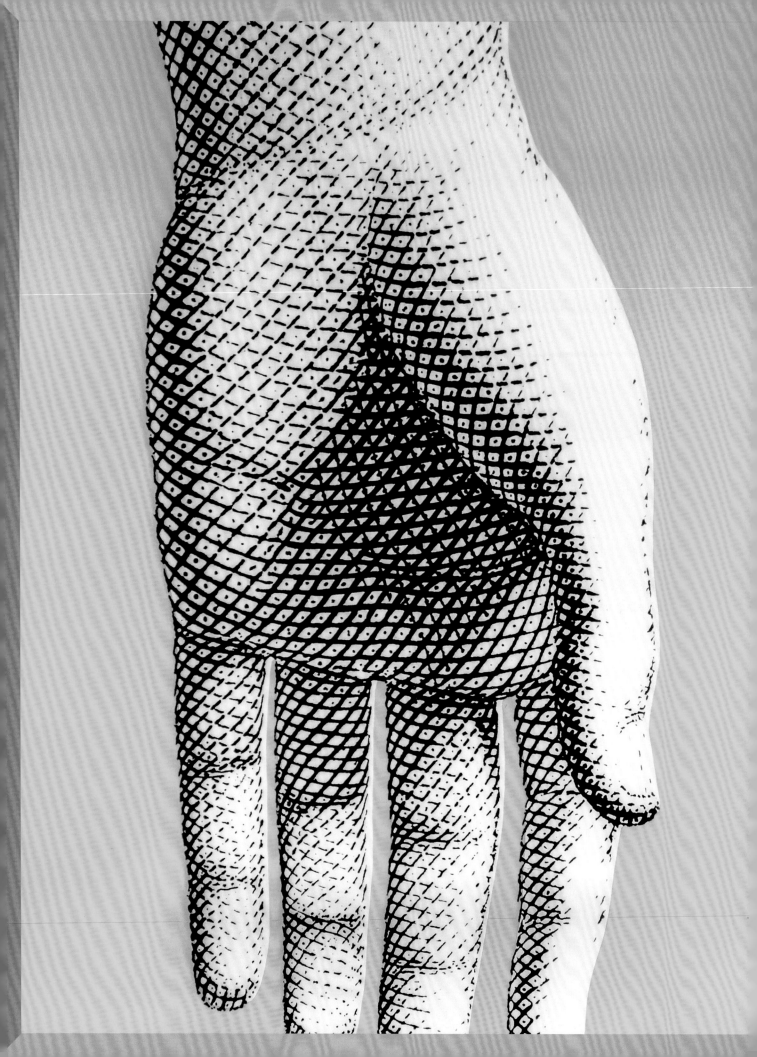

BARNABA FORNASETTI

Casa Fornasetti, Milan

Barnaba Fornasetti was born in his family home in Milan in 1950, the only child of artists Giulia Gelmi and Piero Fornasetti. Almost seventy years later, he still lives at Casa Fornasetti and finds being away from home virtually unbearable. 'I am absolutely addicted to it. My home is a protective oasis in perpetual transformation. It represents my life: my job, my interests and my philosophy – all entwined. All these elements merge into my habitat, which is my dress, my skin, my instrument of communication and sustenance.'

His home is as much a part of Barnaba as his wavy beard and unwavering gaze, but for many years he chose to live elsewhere. After attending Milan's Brera Academy in the 1960s, including a short stint in jail as a result of his participation in left-wing student protests, Barnaba moved away to find his own creative voice. He designed fabrics for fashion designer Ken Scott, restored ancient farmhouses in Tuscany and worked for several years on a music magazine. In 1982, with the fruits of his own creative exploration now ripened, he moved back home to work alongside his father.

Barnaba's parents, Piero and Giulia, were both from deeply traditional Milanese families who were unsupportive of their choices to pursue lives in art and design. They resisted pressure from their families and attended Brera Academy and the Scuola Superiore di Arti Applicate all'Industria. They recognised each other as kindred spirits and later married. Just as they had rejected their families' career expectations, they also rejected the prevailing attitudes and rigid rules of Milanese society, including the elegant sameness and trends in home décor. Emboldened by their union,

they invented a different way of living, centred around boundless creative exploration.

Barnaba remembers that, when he was growing up, the home's work and personal spaces were kept separate. 'My father adapted the building to the needs of his artistic activity. The house was divided into two wings: one being my parents' private quarters, and the other the atelier, which included the offices and the studio, where the entire production cycle would take place.'

Casa Fornasetti was originally built in the late 19th century by Barnaba's grandfather, Pietro Fornasetti. He lived there with his wife, Martha Munch, a German woman known for her passionate, Sicilian-like character. Barnaba's father, Piero, was the eldest of their four children. At that time, the property was in the rural outskirts of Milan, in an area known as Città degli Studi. Now, more than a century later, the area has been swallowed by the anonymous and uninspiring suburban streetscapes characteristic of much of the postwar development in the city.

Like many well-to-do Milanese families, they spent their summers at Lake Como, where Pietro built the two-storey Villa Fornasetti. As a teenager, Piero did not pass his days in a languid rotation of swimming, boating, eating gelati and chasing fireflies, but instead used the time to experiment with paint, pencil and pastel, interpreting the scenes around him. Perhaps believing that his son's talent could be contained as a hobby rather than a career, Pietro gave Piero an area on the ground floor of their home in Milan to do his artwork. He even submitted, along with other family members, for portraits such as *Ritratto di Profile del Padre* (*Profile Portrait of the Artist's Father*, 1927).

A photograph of fourteen-year-old Piero in 1927 shows him standing near a display of twenty-seven of his paintings. He is dressed in a suit and tie with his arms behind his back and has an intense, unsmiling gaze. Even at that young age, Piero worked with seriousness and absolute determination. Later, he used this same approach to defy his authoritarian father, who was determined that his firstborn child should become an accountant and work in the family business, importing typewriters from Germany.

By the time Barnaba was born, Piero was almost forty years old and on his way to becoming one of Italy's most influential designers. His career as an interior decorator, industrial designer, fashion designer, painter, sculptor and engraver ultimately spanned five decades and resulted in the production of approximately 13,000 objects and a fruitful collaboration with architect Gio Ponti.

As a child, Barnaba's sense of 'normal' was very different from that of other Milanese children. 'At first, I did not notice the incredible reality, or better, *surreality* in which I was born. But when I began to compare my surroundings with the others that I happened to visit, I realised how unconventional and unusual the world was that my father created around him, and around me as well.'

Barnaba inherited his father's creative outlook as well as his belief in the benefits of hard work. Piero once said, 'True artists follow a healthy principle: they begin working in the morning and work all day until evening, and they do not wait passively for inspiration to come. They wait for it on the "battlefield", since inspiration comes from working, at a moment that no one can predict.'

Since Piero's death in 1988, Barnaba has designed tableware, rugs, clothing, furniture, CD covers, sets for opera and experimental music performances, guitars, bikes and motorbikes. He also manages the extensive archives left by his father.

After inheriting Casa Fornasetti, Barnaba, like his father before him, changed the interiors to suit his own needs. He reconfigured the layout, and changed the colours and decorative elements. He merged the work and personal spaces into a maze of rooms and corridors that flow over three levels. 'Now the different areas are more integrated: the archive, the creative and communication offices, the meeting room, the library, the music room, my private accommodation and the guest rooms.'

Each room has been anchored with a different colour that gives it a distinctive character and emotional atmosphere. The emerald-green sitting room is dominated by a large feature wall containing twenty-two mirrors, arranged salon-style, every one with a different shape and frame. The play of light created by the mirrors is accentuated by an arched window that Piero installed to display a rainbow array of 19th-century cut-glass Biedermeier goblets on transparent shelves. Many of the mirrors have a story, including the ten-lobed convex mirror designed by Piero in the early 1960s, which was inspired by a mirror in the 1434 painting *Ritratto dei coniugi Arnolfini* (*Portrait of Giovanni Arnolfini and his Wife*) by Flemish artist Jan van Eyck. Another of Piero's mirrors was made with black lacquered wood decorated with seashells, a technique he used to embellish everything from bathrooms to busts.

Shell decorating was a family affair. Barnaba used thousands of shells sent from Venice to adorn the walls of Villa Fornasetti's dining room, a project he completed over two summers. His mother created a shell chandelier to match the walls, which hung above a padauk timber table designed by Piero in 1954.

In an olive-leaf coloured music room on the second floor, the passions of three generations of Fornasetti men are united. Pietro was a keen amateur opera and bel canto singer and he shared his enthusiasm for music with his children. Piero's love of music extended to theatre and performance, and he relished the opportunity to design the sets and costumes for a 1954 production of Gian Carlo Menotti's *Amelia Goes to the Ball* at Milan's famous La Scala theatre.

But the music room is not a museum of the Fornasetti family. It is a playful, party-ready space, with echoes of Barnaba's childhood

> Each room has been anchored with a different colour that gives it a distinctive character and emotional atmosphere.

bedroom where posters of the Beatles adorned the walls along with pictures of cars cut out from magazines. 'Music is my hobby and I have an extensive CD and LP collection, mainly from the 1960s and 70s when I worked on a music magazine.' His tastes include classical, modern and contemporary experimental music. Like his father, Barnaba uses music themes in his designs. In 2007, in a homage to Vivaldi, he designed an area rug called Quattro Stagioni (Four Seasons) that covers much of the music room floor. It depicts a large tree divided into four parts, each representing a different season. On the bottom right, the tree's limbs are virtually bare, with the first signs of spring appearing on the branches above. The top left is in full flowering symphony, exploding into a grand finale of colossal orange pomegranates.

The red guest bedroom in Casa Fornasetti is virtually identical to a room Piero decorated in Villa Fornasetti on Lake Como. Piero explained, 'In a room in which everything is red, from the floor to the walls and the furniture, from the bed to the blanket, soap and toiletries, I put a collection of books. There are already more than 300 of them that have the word "red" in their title.' Barnaba says that guests don't last long in the room, admitting that perhaps the intensity of the colour becomes overwhelming after a few nights.

One of the bigger changes Barnaba made to Casa Fornasetti was enclosing an external portico. It had been used as an outdoor eating area, with hanging plants, a swing seat and iron chairs around a large round table. Barnaba converted it to a kitchen and knocked a hole through the chimney to extend the living room's fireplace into the new room.

In a photograph of the portico taken in the mid-1950s, Piero sits near four large rattan rug beaters. He had them made to mimic the design of the ones Pietro used to beat his children. Working with specialist artisans to create objects of such beauty from what must have been painful memories may have been a cathartic process. It is another demonstration of the nerve he needed to defy his father and live a life free of the constraints of family and society. In the photo,

Piero has the same steely gaze that he had at fourteen. Behind him, a thriving cluster of leafy climbing plants weave up and around the beaters. They seem quietly determined to choose their own path, much like Pietro's four children.

Two walls of Barnaba's kitchen are made up of floor-to-ceiling concertina glass doors. An oversized Murano chandelier hangs above a round white table that is decorated, along with the chairs and floors, with Barnaba's Ultime Notizie (Latest News) designs. Piero's 1938 painting *La Venditrice di Farfalle* (*The Butterfly Seller*) dominates one wall. An abundance of natural light gives the kitchen a bright, airy feel, unlike the rest of the house, which generally has smaller windows. The visual interchange between indoors and outdoors is most apparent in this room.

The large internal courtyard garden at Casa Fornasetti is as vital to the personality of the property today as it was when Barnaba's grandparents lived there. In a photo of the family taken in the 1920s, Pietro and Martha stand on a central pathway that leads to the house, with their children on a balcony behind them. At that time, the garden was dominated by fruit trees and vegetables that grew in neat rows or were trained to climb up wooden stakes.

When Piero inherited the property soon after World War II, he created a classical Italian garden with fruit-bearing medlar, persimmon and apricot trees, hedges of pittosporum and hydrangeas, fragrant wisteria climbers and a willow tree that provided a central point of focus. These days the garden has a more rambling, unstructured feel.

Photographing Barnaba on the couch in his music room, surrounded by the objects that he and his father created, it feels for a moment like time has stopped. As he adjusts his position, centring himself between a magnificent convex mirror and a series of framed drawings, his eyes lock in a direct gaze to the camera. For a moment, father and son are one. Barnaba's bold and fearless expression is identical to his father's, captured in that portrait at Lake Como ninety years before. ◆

MILLE & UNE

The Museum and the Fairy's Den

Seventeen years ago, an ornate crown was discovered in France. The crown wasn't made with gold and priceless gems and pearls, but with paper, cardboard and wire. When Valerie Mille saw it, she felt compelled to find its creator, artist Claire Guiral. Without the crown, the friendship that changed the course of both their lives would never have begun.

Despite the two women moving in vastly different circles and living in contrasting circumstances, 500 kilometres apart, they immediately recognised each other as kindred spirits. 'We were like two old ladies, but still dreaming like little girls,' Claire says about their 2001 meeting. They have now formed a collaboration they call Mille & Une, which has culminated in the conversion of an 18th-century apartment into the most secret and private museum in Paris.

When Claire was young, she wanted to be a fairy. As an adult, she lives as close to her childhood imaginings as she can, without the obvious benefits of wings and a magic wand. She has created a home that resembles a fairy den. Here, she toils away making crowns and tiny dresses from paper and wire for imaginary sovereigns, jewellery from corrugated cardboard, and elaborate miniature papier-mâché scenes with fully dressed mice, flying mermaids, gentlemen in top hats, and tiny ladies sitting on *Princess and the Pea* beds with a tower of mattresses. Her walls are painted in blues, teals and soft creams, and the cushions are made from hand-dyed fabrics in dusty shades of pink and orange. Each room has been furnished with an assortment of vintage, handmade and antique furniture, providing a stage for the display of her work.

She occupies the first floor of the home she once shared with her husband, Philippe, and their son, Philemon, in the historic French port town of Bordeaux. When the couple separated amicably six years ago, Claire and Philemon moved upstairs and Philippe took over the ground floor. They began a different way of living, which involved accepting each other's lovers and co-parenting in an organic, upstairs–downstairs kind of way. Their friends thought the arrangement could not possibly work. Yet it does.

Claire works in virtual anonymity in her cosy little quarters. Built in 1887, her home has several architectural elements typical of the *échoppe bordelaise* style. 'From the outside, it looks like a city house but from the inside it is more like a house in the countryside because of the colours and decoration.' On the back of each door hangs one of her creations, such as a paper dress flanked by golden papercuts and a multicoloured handmade coat lined with fuchsia and burgundy striped silk. Necklaces in tertiary tones line the balustrade at the top of the stairs and tumble like a waterfall over a bucket chair. Her four-poster bed is wrapped in soft tulle and muslin, littered with silk flowery cushions, and draped with a large scarf of fine wool. She has set up a daybed in the corner of her tiny workroom and a green wooden lorikeet watches over everything from the centre of the room. 'I think that if you placed me in a white, very clean apartment with a lot of plastic, I would die very quickly.'

Valerie lives in Brittany, five hours north of Claire. She has also always preferred to live with one foot in a dreamscape, an approach that began in childhood and has been maintained throughout her adult life. When she was a child, Valerie wanted to be a princess. She imagined a life of beautiful gowns, crowns and palaces, devoid of the dullness of reality. When she grew up she married Richard Mille, a French luxury watchmaker. They purchased Château Monbouan, an 18th-century castle set on a sprawling rural estate. Valerie wears long ornate dresses with hems that sweep the floor as she walks. She has large, curious eyes and speaks in a soft lyrical voice about colour and fabric and art and beauty.

Seventeen years after Valerie's first conversation with Claire, she still remembers the immediacy of their personal connection. Valerie began to buy and commission work from Claire. She also began collecting crowns, which she displays like sculptures on mantles and antique tables. As their friendship developed, Valerie came up with an extraordinary plan. She told Claire she wanted to purchase a property in Paris with the sole purpose of converting it into a museum to showcase Claire's work to the world. Valerie's children had grown up and she had more time, so she thought 'now I can take care of Claire'. Claire was thrilled with the idea and Valerie purchased an apartment in the 17th arrondissement, facing Parc Monceau on the Right Bank.

Valerie engaged Philippe Breton to help her convert the apartment 'into a fairy tale'. Each room is decorated like scenes from a whimsical play. Jewels, crowns, brooches and paper flowers inhabit each space. White birds with long sweeping tails have been handpainted on grey flannel-toned walls in the bureau, and the entrance vestibule is covered with gold leaf. Inside the pale-mint ballroom, on a large semicircular carousel, hang thirty-five paper dresses complete with little paper shoes, bags, scarves and hats. Dozens of papier-mâché balls are positioned on the floor in the parlour, as though rolled there during a game of giant marbles.

Valerie and Claire have a similar feel for colour and the colours in the Paris museum mirror those of Claire's home in Bordeaux. Claire's affinity for colour began when she was seven, in her grandmother's home in France. She recalls a rich turquoise hue which covered the climbing vines in the garden, thanks to a fungicide spray known as 'Bordeaux mixture'. Inside the house, red wallpaper with white, grey and gold flowers covered the walls, and beds were swathed in green and orange velvet blankets.

At the same time that Claire began learning the language of colour, she also recognised that she was very happy spending time on her own. She did not search out human company, preferring to talk to her grandmother's five rabbits who had warm-grey coloured coats and lived in the garden down a little path made of old broken tiles. When she needed an escape from her grandmother's attempts at conversation, she hid in a small cabinet under the staircase and read her favourite fairy tales by lamplight. Reading *Cinderella*, she felt a strong connection with the fairy and her ability to turn a pumpkin into a beautiful carriage and the dress of a pauper into the dress of a princess.

The transformation of basic things into magical objects and scenes became her goal. 'I was a very fancy little girl who wanted to create.' She began to make ornate objects and dresses from simple materials. A curtain became an elaborate party dress, complete with a long train, and cardboard offcuts became jewellery. Her parents viewed Claire and her creations with kind bewilderment, and treated her as the 'beloved alien' in the family. Claire approaches her adult life like an extended childhood in which imagination is the key to living. She continues to convert simple materials into beautiful things, which now live in the private collections of clients and loyal followers.

> The tiny private museum in Paris ... is a testament to a mutually supportive and creatively fuelled friendship ...

The tiny private museum in Paris that showcases Claire's work to like-minded people by private appointment is a testament to a mutually supportive and creatively fuelled friendship that, in some ways, resembles the traditional roles of patron and artist. Looked at another way, it's a magical friendship between a princess and a fairy, who helped to transport each other into a world that neither of them could have created on her own. While they each have their own homes, this is their shared fairytale home, the home of their ideas and artistry, which they can also share with a small group of lucky visitors from around the world. ◆

J MORGAN PUETT

Forest Farmhouse

As children, J Morgan Puett and her siblings would form a little assembly line on the back porch of the family home in Georgia, USA, and make tiny wooden cages for queen bees. One child would staple cellophane and wire onto the frame, another would make sugar dough for the queen bee to feed on, then another plugged the end of the cage with cork. Their father, Garnett Puett, a fourth-generation beekeeper, would place each queen bee into its new home and ship the miniature packages to apiarists around America.

Garnett's specialty was breeding and grafting queen bees. Through a lens of social consciousness, he taught his children important practical and philosophical lessons about the systems of cooperation and labour inside the bee colonies. Almost fifty years later, Morgan (as she prefers to be called) still recalls the quiet magic of those moments. 'Some of my fondest memories were working with my father, learning biology through the process of grafting little bee grubs in a shack in the pine forest.'

Morgan's mother was a painter. She created a small school in the abandoned house next door that she called Beehive Arts. Three of the four Puett children went on to keep their own bees, including Morgan's brother, Garnett (junior), who runs a bee farm in Hawaii. He also exhibits 'apisculptures' of metal and beeswax, which he makes in collaboration with thousands of bees. For Morgan, the beekeeper's lessons helped foster a utopian outlook, eventually leading to the purchase of a ninety-six-acre property, Mildred's Lane, with two friends and her then partner, Mark Dion. Located among deciduous forests in north-eastern Pennsylvania, Mildred's Lane is set on a gentle slope that leads down to the Delaware River, which separates the State of New York from Pennsylvania.

Mildred's Lane is over 1600 kilometres from Georgia, where Morgan was born in 1957. She grew up in a time and place mired in the social upheaval and violence of the civil rights movement. At home, her parents fostered an environment where ideas, politics, art, music and creative industry thrived. Publicly, they faced social castigation because of Garnett's outspoken opposition to racial oppression and his support of the abolition of racial segregation. While the flames of hatred burnt through Georgia and beyond, Garnett educated his children about the ideals of peaceful living and cooperation, using bee colonies as an example. This exchange of ideas ended abruptly in 1971 when Garnett died. Morgan was thirteen years old.

In her adult life, she has consciously worked to recapture the creative essence of her childhood. Mildred's Lane provides her with unlimited opportunities to play grown-up versions of her favourite childhood games, form a community around new projects and ideas, and recreate Puett family interests like boatbuilding and, of course, beekeeping. 'Remember the natural collaboration we had in our childhoods? Nobody asked the question, "Who's the author?" We just went at it. "Project! Fort!" Everybody authored it, everybody built it, and we were all proudly involved. That's the quality of life I seek at Mildred's Lane.'

Large-scale assignments, sometimes involving dozens of collaborators, unfold at Mildred's Lane in a seasonal tide. The property itself feels like one large installation, and the art practices that take place there defy normal categorisation. It functions as a home, but also has temporary accommodation for artists and students; it's an archaeology site and also a vast forest retreat and artists' workshop. Morgan describes it as a gathering place for like-minded people to collectively redefine the way they live, create and engage with each other and the environment. 'It is a home and an experiment in living; reassembling the connections between working, living, and researching through contemporary concepts and projects sensitive to the site.'

Boundaries are blurred between work and play, and practice and creativity. Many of the projects born at Mildred's Lane marry a playful lightness with serious creative exploration. Artists Clayton Lewis and Christine Buckley collaborated with Morgan on the 2012 installation exhibition, *MoMA Studio: Common Senses*, by creating small vials of *The Artist's Elixir – The Ideal Immortality Tonic* from fungi found at Mildred's Lane. The tiny bottles were offered for sale, with an attached note that read 'Ever-lasting ingenuity guaranteed!' and 'Crafted and bottled exclusively at MoMA for Mildred's Lane – beware of imitations, avoid substitutes'.

The simplest of tasks are elevated to performance art at Mildred's Lane. Beekeeping, meal-making and what Morgan calls house-hooshing (creating installations) are all approached with a mixture of urgency and amusement. Three Czech artists arrived one rainy night to plant an array of native flowering plants for Morgan's bees, then made a small monetary donation and stayed for drinks on the deck followed by philosophical conversation over one of Morgan's beautifully staged and lovingly prepared home-cooked dinners. Social Saturdays usually involve large-scale outdoor dining events, set up as installations, featuring the work of any number of visiting artists. Artist Amy Yoes is a regular. Her work involves the creation and ritual burning of magnificent wood and paper sculptures, and the subsequent bottling of the remaining charcoal for artists' use.

There are also several long-term projects. *Mildred Archaeology II* (ongoing since 1998) involves the collective digging of a 20th-century garbage dump and the exhibition of the finds in all their rusty, broken, mud-stained glory. There is also an annual calendar of workshops, such as *Wasting, Wilding, Workstyling II* (2017), a collaboration between Morgan and Athena Kokoronis 'with visiting artists, local naturalists, gardeners, botanists, beekeepers to workshop

topics such as beekeeping, collecting, pressing, tincturing, planting, mycoremediation, soil biology – wildcrafting'.

Visitors are invited to rethink traditional hierarchies and relationships between teachers, students, artists and institutions. 'Mildred's Lane is a school about living, and not just in linear terms, it's a swarming ... a complex. It's a complexity.' Static and conventional roles are consciously collapsed and reconsidered, and often replaced with a fluid, democratic model that Morgan describes as 'a revolutionary, rigorous rethinking (the three Rs) of the contemporary art complex'.

There are a number of buildings on the property, including the home Morgan designed and where she lives with her son Grey Rabbit Puett (known as Rabbit). Visiting artists who stay there include Rabbit's father, Mark Dion. Other buildings that punctuate the landscape include the c. 1830 farmhouse called Mildred's House, and a cluster of rustic wooden cottages. Morgan explains that, while the little outbuildings on the property 'have a 19th-century vernacular, the ideas and theories and the voices that move through here are contemporary. They are made by very forward-thinking creative practitioners. That is a bee colony. That is a beehive.'

Each building and every room is an ever-changing embodiment of Morgan's work, often conducted with collaborators. It is part of her broader vision and she invites visitors to engage in and reconsider 'the feminist driven task of creative, inventive domesticating: how one moves through the day, not merely as an artist through their studio, but as a person in their environment, dealing with all the special and political entanglements of every aspect of life'. One of the most majestic structures on the property is a treehouse that was built in conjunction with artist Scott Constable in 2000, in honour of Rabbit's birth. It was later struck by lightning, which destroyed its leaves and any colour in

> Garnett ... taught his children important practical and philosophical lessons about the systems of cooperation and labour inside the bee colonies.

its branches or trunk. It now stands like a pale wooden skeleton, framed against the dark green foliage of the woods beyond.

All of the collaboratively built structures at Mildred's Lane are art installations. Morgan sees the spaces as 'a living system. You can live in the installations.' *The Grafter's Shack* (2002) has special meaning. It was inspired by her father's queen bee grafting hut. The original building was set alight and burnt, along with the precious beehives, by right-wing opponents of her father's political views. Garnett was a radical white man from an established family in the Deep South, and the family's personal property was sometimes destroyed for his outspoken stance. 'He was constantly conflicted in dealing with his world as a liberal man living in the south. During political seasons his bee yards would get burnt down. Seeing these charred beehives really affected me. One of my most traumatic memories as a child was going to see my daddy's bee yards burnt.'

She remembers his passion for standing up for what he believed in. He wrote letters to the newspaper and ran for government. She also remembers his grassroots approach to engaging in dialogue, including his Sunday morning ritual of taking beans and chili into Black communities and discussing ways to help them organise.

Like her father, Morgan uses food and the table as important elements of her work. They are a platform for the exchange of ideas, and the birthplace of projects and collaborations. She also sees herself as a custodian of the land and explains she is like an ambassador, 'not to the A-R-T word – I am an Ambassador of Entanglement rather than artist, curator, director, architect, or other. I am an ambassador to my landscape project, my environment and my interests in the little bewilderness of Mildred's Lane.'

She offers Mildred's Lane as a place for people 'to experience the landscape, to become more sensitive to the environment, engage with the world of both human and non-human'. Rather than sidelining domestic tasks in order to make time for her creative work, she believes

'life *is* our work … domesticity *is* an intellectually creative and vital experience, rich with rhetoric of aesthetics, arranging labour, sociality, politics and more. These are aesthetic systems that are forms of political engagement with one's surroundings.'

Stepping inside the large metal cage that was built to protect her beehives from bears, Morgan senses my concern as swarms of bees begin a feverish dance around us. With neither of us wearing protective garb, I am wondering if it was such a good idea to photograph Morgan with her bees. 'Just move very, very slowly,' she says quietly. I stop walking, remain completely still, and just listen. Soon the hum of the bees forms a single, gentle and mesmerising voice that has its own hypnotic frequency. Fear dissolves and is replaced with a surprising feeling of absolute peace as I begin to photograph the tender exchange between the beekeeper and her bees, and marvel at the home they have created together. ◆

FRANCESCO CLEMENTE

Home of the Nomad

It's tea time at artist Francesco Clemente's studio in New York and he carries out the tea ceremony with quiet intensity. 'I treat it like a meditation.' He places two small finely crafted porcelain cups and a Chinese teapot on a wooden tray, breaks a corner from a compressed tea brick and allows it time to steep in water. 'Pu'er tea is the best. It's literally fermented for ten, fifteen or twenty years. There's a way to make Pu'er tea - it's called the "awakening of the tea". You don't drink the first pour.'

Francesco moved from Italy to New York in 1981 with his wife Alba and their two children. Looking for a place to live and work, he was shown a vast warehouse space in a dilapidated building on Broadway, which was 'the second most dangerous street in New York. Only Bond Street was more dangerous.' Francesco found it deeply appealing. 'Everything I liked was here: crime; stylised, interesting types; and it was also fantastically inexpensive.' He bought the practically derelict loft and moved in with his family. 'It used to be a fancy showroom at the turn of the 19th century and then this section of Broadway was abandoned when all the great shops and theatres moved uptown. It became a place of factories and small manufacturers.' As the factories moved out, artists moved in. Francesco was one of the first, along with Jean-Michel Basquiat who lived around the corner, and the two artists became firm friends.

Francesco and Alba's loft soon became a magnet for an eclectic mix of artists, musicians, writers and designers. Italian architect and industrial designer Ettore Sottsass made several pieces of furniture for them including their bed, a mirror, and a small side table. 'Three pieces that are to

me the sum of what you need in life.' They bought chairs, a couch, a shelf and another small table designed by Frank Lloyd Wright. That was a time when 'you could get his furniture for a few hundred dollars a piece'. Artist Julian Schnabel created their large dining table – 'the first piece of furniture he ever made' – and its iron frame was so long that a crane was needed to lift it through the window. The table became the setting for Alba's legendary meals, and details of their dinner parties are recorded in Andy Warhol's diaries.

Francesco and Alba's friends visited each other's studios, gathered around each other's dining tables, and were often the subjects of each other's paintings and photographs. Francesco and Basquiat painted each other; Basquiat painted Warhol; Alba was painted by Francesco, Basquiat, Alex Katz and Kenny Scharf. Warhol photographed Francesco, Alba and Basquiat. Robert Mapplethorpe, who was godfather to one of Francesco and Alba's children, photographed Francesco, Alba, Warhol and virtually every other artist in New York. In 1984, Francesco and Basquiat joined forces with Warhol to create an exhibition where they each worked in turn on the same canvases. One of their collaborative works, *Alba's Breakfast* (1984), features Alba serving eggs, bacon and coffee to several hungry and wild-looking visitors, just as she often did.

Francesco's collaborations never threatened his sense of self, partly because he is interested in the Buddhist concept of 'non-self'. 'I really don't want to call myself anything, I don't want to be anyone really. I think disappearing is the ultimate achievement.' Francesco is not constrained by cultural, social or geographical boundaries, nor defined by any religion. He does not identify with any particular art movement and, with the exception of being regarded as a nomad, he rejects labels of almost every kind. 'I'm not a partisan of any particular belief, there are enough divisions in the world as it is.'

One of his most enduring collaborations was with writer Raymond Foye. In 1986, they formed Hanuman Books and produced limited edition, pocket-size handmade books inspired by Hare Krishna prayer books. They published more than fifty titles by artists, writers and photographers, including Robert Creeley, Allen Ginsberg, Gregory Corso, Robert Frank, René Daumal, Simone Weil and Henri Michaux. They also published the writing of visual and performing artists such as David Hockney, Patti Smith and Willem de Kooning.

He has also collaborated with miniaturists and master tentmakers in India, designed album covers for Mick Jagger, produced paintings for a film by Mexican director Alfonso Cuarón, worked on joint projects with poet Allen Ginsberg and author Salman Rushdie, painted portraits of supermodels for *Harper's Bazaar*, and worked on an exhibition with New York's Metropolitan Opera.

Hanging on walls, sitting on shelves and clustered around a shrine Francesco has set up in his studio are mementoes of these collaborations along with artwork from friends, including two works by Basquiat. 'I love the fact that this work is on found metal. It was still on the edge between what he was doing on the streets and what he was doing in the studio.' A collection of miniature Hanuman books sits on a little wooden display shelf, near a framed photograph of Ramana Maharshi, an ascetic whose teaching was silence. 'I am very fond of him. He was a well-known figure in the 1940s and 50s in southern India. He lived very simply in a small village. He never said anything, he just left the so-called "30 Verses of Wisdom".'

Francesco's life in New York was vastly different to the lives of his parents. He was born in Naples, Italy, in 1952, the only child of Bianca Quarto and aristocrat Marquese Lorenzo Clemente di San Luca. By his late teenage years, he decided to leave behind his conservative upbringing and explore another way of living. He moved to Rome to study architecture and met a number of artists from the Arte Povera (poor art) movement. 'I come from a Marxist-educated, anti-capitalist generation and the failure of that point of view led me to look for an entirely different scenario.

I decided to abandon history, and embrace geography, to find my answers in non-Western scenarios where the dialectic of the West was not so important.'

In 1974, he travelled to Afghanistan with his friend and mentor, Alighiero e Boetti, an Italian conceptual artist who was ten years his senior. They followed the ancient Silk Road by truck across the dramatic and isolated Pamir and Hindu Kush mountain ranges to the Chinese border and up to the northern city of Feyzabad on the Kokcha River. Francesco was well outside his comfort zone, and in that discomfort he found the beginnings of a nomadic life.

Emboldened by his travels with Boetti and inspired by his artwork, Francesco proceeded to India. He has lived and worked in Rajasthan, Varanasi and Chennai for extended periods ever since. 'I'm very fond of the Hindu imagination. It's a fantastic world – particularly from an iconographic point of view.' While he is not a partisan to any particular belief, his sensibility leans towards Hindu and Buddhist traditions. The shrine he has set up in his studio includes a collection of deities, wooden tantric objects and a trunk filled with small toys. 'That is very important, first of all because one of the important deities is baby Krishna who plays with toys, and also because play is important in all of these traditions … In the West, when we think of worship we think of falling on our knees and crying and pulling our hair out. A devotee of Krishna thinks of jumping up, singing a song, playing a musical instrument and dancing.'

Letting go of fear is key to his preparation to work. 'I'm very fond of a place where you are confronted by the whole picture of life, because you don't have to imagine it, and make it worse than what it is. You just see it, you see life and death and that's what it is. It's very liberating. It liberates me from my fears. I would not be an artist if I wasn't fantastically aware of death. You can't make anything if you are in the grip of fear.'

> By his late teenage years, he decided to leave behind his conservative upbringing and explore another way of living.

This is one of the reasons he is drawn to Varanasi and the Ganges River, which flows along its outskirts. 'Varanasi is a very tough place because it's where people go to die. It's where the pure and the impure mix, which means you'll see a corpse burning, and next to it a bunch of children playing cricket, and next to that somebody washing their clothes. It's everything jumbled together in this extraordinary spectacle. But it's not a spectacle for everyone.' While some travellers turn away from the burning funeral pyres and scenes of poverty, Francesco moves towards them and his fears are absolved.

Francesco now lives and works between India, Italy, New Mexico and New York, with occasional stints in China, Brazil and Jamaica. He has also strengthened his roots in New York. In the late 1980s, he began using the Broadway loft only as a studio, and bought a 19th-century townhouse on MacDougal Street in Greenwich Village to live in with his family. The house, which used to belong Bob Dylan, backs onto a private garden that is shared by twenty-one homes on MacDougal and Sullivan streets. The four Clemente children grew up roaming safely in the garden. They celebrated their birthdays and Halloween there, chased fireflies in July, and disappeared in and out of the neighbours' houses on unstructured, casual playdates. Despite its low-key, casually maintained feel, it is one of the most famous hidden gardens in New York. Its reputation is fuelled as much by its inaccessibility as the names of those who do have access, which have included Anna Wintour, Richard Gere and Baz Luhrmann. The garden is also the setting for Salman Rushdie's latest novel *The Golden House* (2017), which he began writing after spending time at the Clementes' home.

So, does MacDougal Street feel like home for Francesco? He is very fond of the home and its artwork and objects, but he only feels comfortable *not* belonging. He actively seeks discomfort and appreciates the value of boredom and unease as catalysts for new ideas and new work. 'The strategy of my work is nomadic. I spend my life trying to displace myself, displace my views, displace my point of view and find myself in between places. The fact that I have more than one place in different locales, in different

countries, really has to do with the organisational side of that idea.' Like a ship's captain, he often anchors in New York, but he never stays for long.

He denies himself a definitive home, but simultaneously yearns for one, and the resulting nostalgia feeds into his work. Nomadic thinking also extends to constant changes in art media. He creates paintings, prints, collages, monotypes, mosaics, photographs, wax frescoes, fabric installations and sculptures. He works with watercolour, wood, gouache, pencil, pastel, ink, oils, cotton, canvas fabric and silk. His work is like a complex jigsaw puzzle; he explores and sometimes merges diverse cultural, theoretical, spiritual and allegorical symbols. He draws inspiration from poetry, literature, music, art history, popular culture and film and works in collections – or constellations as he prefers to call them – developing and growing with, and through, an idea.

It is the unknown in the creative process that is important to Francesco. 'Painting is interesting as it leads you to places you don't know. I think I am fortunate as I am unable to control the final outcome of what I do. I begin with one image in mind and end up in an entirely new place.' In order to create the right psychological environment for a narrative to emerge he prepares his mind. 'I prepare by getting unprepared. So I make room for intuitive process and then after that I see what place it has in a general picture.'

He believes in the benefits of meditation, contemplation and yoga, and he commits fully to every painting, every tea ceremony and every moment like the true master that he is. ◆

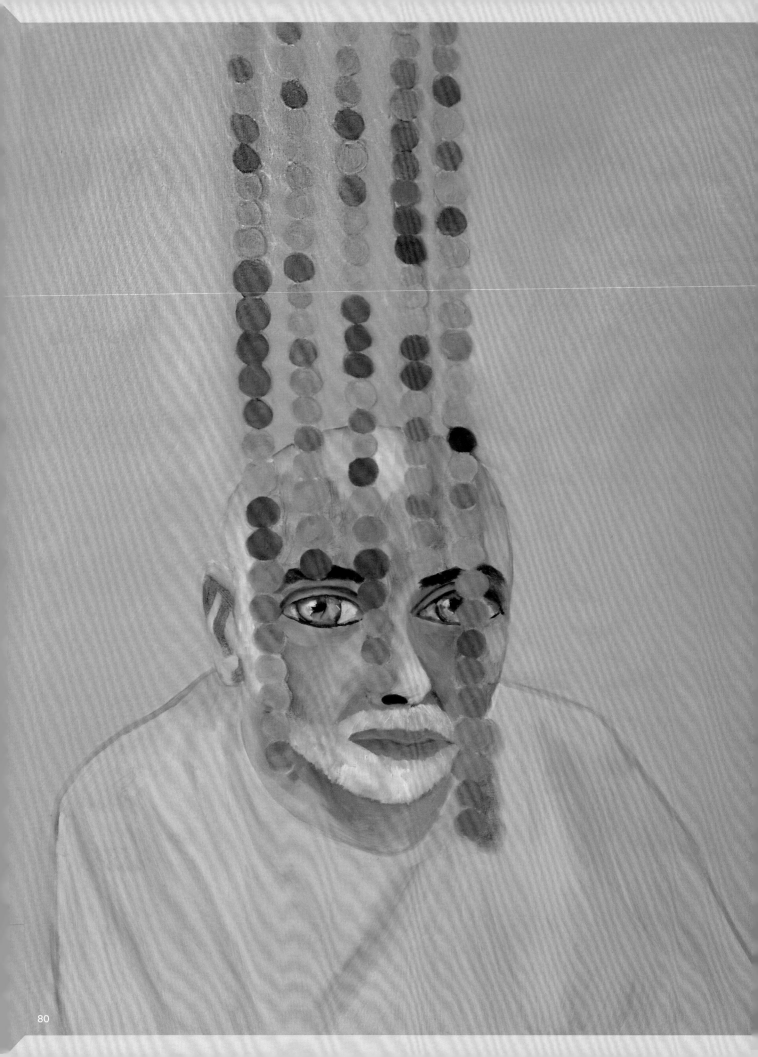

JOSHUA YELDHAM

Into the Nest

When Joshua Yeldham was eight, he was sent to an all-boys boarding school, located just ten minutes from his home in Sydney, Australia. The shock of leaving the security of the family home and the mother he adored, was immediate and traumatic. The feeling of dislocation was compounded by being deposited into a sea of schoolboys and becoming a target for the cruellest of them. 'I didn't tell my mum I was having my head shoved in a toilet and cockroaches put in my bed.'

Undiagnosed dyslexia, coupled with the corporal punishment meted out by several teachers, meant that his experience of his new home was characterised by emotional and physical pain, acute loneliness and fear. He needed a safe place. 'The bullies didn't come in the art room, so I hung out there.'

These early experiences left Joshua with a furious energy that he later exorcised in forests, rivers, deserts and some of the highest mountain peaks in the world. They were also processed through his artwork, which has catapulted him to great heights in Australian contemporary art. He is now one of the most accomplished artists of his generation. 'You find a link with a lot of artists – what I had to do was build, I call it a ladder, out of resistance.'

Joshua lives and works in Pittwater, north of Sydney, with his photographer wife, Jo Yeldham, and their two children, Indigo and Jude. The home comprises three interconnected parts: their boat, *Victory*; the bushland and mangroves that line the nearby Pittwater estuary and Hawkesbury River; and their airy and inviting 19th-century weatherboard house.

Their house is filled with artwork, photographs and personal treasures. There are views of their lush garden from almost all its rooms, and glimpses of the estuary from the deck. Animals, rocks, eucalypts and subtropical plants frame their property and populate the landscape around them. Joshua has found a constant source of subject matter for his work. He has also found his spiritual home.

When Joshua was a child, his family owned a hobby farm near the Hawkesbury River. On weekends away from boarding school, he got to know the people who lived by the river. He was drawn to these river dwellers, and later to mountain men, desert nomads and artists.

One of his early male role models was his martial arts teacher, Gary. As well as teaching eleven-year-old Joshua how to defend himself against his classmates, Gary also helped him to overcome his fears. 'He took me out after homework and we were jumping off things and climbing in the darkness.'

When he was fourteen, after a particularly disturbing episode of bullying, Joshua was finally released from boarding school. The timing coincided with his parents' divorce and Joshua moved to London with his mother. He went to board at Aiglon College in Switzerland.

Here, everything was different. Almost all aspects of his education were held in union with nature. There were regular mountain expeditions, stargazing assignments, and three whole-school meditation sessions every week. Joshua learnt perseverance, endurance and adaptability, 'so that I could change tack quickly and go in a different direction. I wanted that freedom. I wanted freedom from hating myself.'

Joshua healed among the pine trees and alpine peaks. On the mountain, the stars and moon shone more brightly, and the dramatic outline of Mont Blanc was a daily reminder of the power and beauty of the natural world. A sense of connection with new friends and wonder at the environment began to replace fear and isolation. 'I felt free from failure in the classroom, free from repetition.

I grew to like myself when I walked along a path through the forest or up a mountain.'

Joshua's art teacher at Aiglon encouraged his love of music, drawing and design. Joshua was fascinated by the animals, trees, snow and ice. At the summit of each mountain, he found another piece of himself. He credits this time in the mountains for showing him how to push through his limits and build a sturdy path to joy.

School holidays fuelled his imagination further. They included wanderings with his family through North Africa, across the Atlas Mountains into Morocco and Algeria. In Paris, he explored the world of art by day, and slept in a run-down river boat on the Seine at night. His knowledge was deepened, his creative voice was strengthened and he was ready to fly.

In 1989, Joshua was accepted into one of the most highly regarded fine art and design institutions in the world, the Rhode Island School of Design in Providence. He fell under the spell of Alfred DeCredico. Joshua vividly recalls the time he and several other students were first invited to Alfred's home, which he shared with his wife Jessan and their two children. The interiors were decorated with a tangle of artworks and artefacts, including handwoven kilims and African masks, sculptures and drums. The students were served a seafood bisque for dinner and opera played in the background. Joshua was captivated by the way that Alfred's family were so entwined in his creative life. The couple's children ran in a riot of energy around the house and studio, and Alfred demonstrated that it was possible to work despite disruptions. 'He painted in a field of riches. His family was vital to his imagery. When I met Jo, all that awareness of Alfred and his wife and children and art – and that it could all happen from a home – it all came flooding through me again, like "I could do this!"'

Observing Alfred also helped Joshua make a conscious choice about how he could experience life as a man and as an artist. 'I'm not going to become bitter, I'm going to become expansive. I'm going to be patient and grow at a solid pace, like a fig tree – just build my trunk, so that even with rejection, I still have my core stability.' Having experienced the negative effects of male aggression, he chose to funnel his own energy in a constructive and disciplined way. 'I want rituals where I can play drums, and shoot arrows, and release the male aggression in me.'

Joshua shifted gear from fine art to moving pictures, combining his love of nature, music, photography and narrative into a semi-autobiographical film, *Frailejon*, which won an Emmy for Best Student Film in America, an Oscar nomination for the Best Student Motion Picture, and led to a Queen's Trust grant and peer and industry recognition.

> Having experienced the negative effects of male aggression, he chose to funnel his own energy in a constructive and disciplined way.

After graduating, he returned to Australia and embarked on solo trips across some of its loneliest and most unforgiving terrain. On one trip, he drove a Volkswagen kombi van from Sydney across the Blue Mountains then followed the 5,614-kilometre fence that was built to keep wild dingoes out of sheep-grazing country. As he slept outdoors, with no walls or ceilings, his internal home and creative terrain expanded. 'My greatest challenge was to build a bridge between myself and the landscape.' Surrounded by endless desert vistas, he felt intensely alive and learnt to dance on a platform of solitude.

On another trip, he created a painting studio in an abandoned 1952 double-decker Leyland he found in the desert, sharing it for forty-two days with grey and orange zebra finches and a timid white-faced barn owl. Art formed the bridge he was searching for and his emotional and spiritual connection to the land became unbreakable. He learnt to listen closely to the songs and warnings of animals. He observed their ecosystems, behaviours and growth cycles, which he later used as themes in his work. Snakes are a recurring symbol in his work and he confronts his fear of them in his paintings. He has deep respect for their ability to transform and he often speaks of metaphorically shedding his own skin in order to grow.

In 1997, Jo and Joshua began to go on desert trips together, culminating in a two-year period when they lived in the kombi van. The experience helped them realise that living a simple life was something they could always return to and that they wanted to face life's challenges together.

Two years after Jo and Joshua were married, they were told that Joshua was infertile. He processed his feelings and experiences through devotional art, looking to subjects in nature and integrating several new techniques into the work. Gallerist Scott Livesey explained the origins of one of these techniques, in which Joshua hammered hundreds of tiny sticks into masonite board paintings. 'Along the central coast and Hawkesbury there is an abundance of oyster farms … In 2005, a devastating disease wiped out much of the industry, turning these farms into graveyards. Joshua saw a metaphor for his own infertility and that's where the stick-work first started.' He also began gouging marks into his work, and making and engraving heavy-gauged, handmade paper. Scott explains further: 'Joshua worked on masonite boards that allowed him to carve, shape and add to the surface, not unlike the erosion and formation of the land itself. And although the paintings are gentle and feel time honoured, the carving is a very brutal and robust process – very loud. He is courageous and I think he will be a giant of his day.'

Joshua chose the owl as a recurring symbol, like a totem. He painted and carved it in a large series of works in the hope that he and Jo might be granted a child. He also began incorporating musical instruments into the prayer-like works, their strings pulled taut across the images. The results were paintings that could be 'played' – musical and visual offerings to nature, like spiritual imaginings of new life.

The owl answered his call. Indigo was born in 2003, followed four years later by Jude. Like their parents, the children live in communion with the water and the forest and are fluent in the language of nature. They name trees, rocks, animals and even the tiniest insects, considering them like members of their extended family. Joshua also counsels his children on the importance of stillness. He can be found at various points in the day in a chair with his eyes closed, deep in meditation. Suddenly chatter in the house falls away and a deeper, more resonant, inner voice emerges to navigate Joshua and his family through their world.

During periods of intense painting, Joshua sometimes goes out alone on the boat for a week at a time. He often travels with a recent owl carving or painting to keep him company, like a friend or mentor. 'My great owl sits up high and sees the land and knows the rustle of all creatures though their alphabet of noise.' He paints on the boat's deck, or by the mangrove creeks, or standing between large boulders. Sometimes he rolls up his work and climbs the riverbank, going deep into the forest to paint on a makeshift frame. He feels like part of the landscape, not separate from it, and trusts that nature will guide and protect him.

Joshua and Jo have created a home where a fluid creative dialogue mirrors the physical movement of family members between the house and studio, boat and land, water and forest. 'I don't think of my studio as sacred. Sacred sometimes means a space you can't perform in. The children have grown up on the floor. It's theirs – with their scissors and glue – it's their space and has been from day one.'

Joshua and Jo have taught their children that creativity can be one of their most reliable friends, supporting them as they explore their place in the world and discover the true meaning of home. ◆

> During periods of intense painting, Joshua sometimes goes out alone on the boat for a week at a time.

JEFFREY JENKINS

Catskills Cottage

Walking through the Raleigh Flea Market at the Historic State Fairgrounds near his home in North Carolina, sixteen-year-old Jeffrey Jenkins spotted a small, chestnut-coloured toy lion. It was damaged and most of its faux fur had worn away. Its broken jaw hung loose and tape was still stuck to the back of its head – evidence of an attempted repair job. The defunct winding mechanism was probably once used to make the lion's mouth roar, amusing its original owner for a short time until it broke. The repair job was unsuccessful, and the toy was replaced by another.

For Jeffrey, the reasons the toy was discarded were the same reasons he was drawn to it. 'I think anything that starts expressing its individuality when it comes from a culture of sameness is interesting. Whoever made that toy probably made a thousand of them, or more. But the one that I found had a broken jaw that had been taped, so there's that empathetic reaction, an anthropomorphic feeling like: "Oh, poor thing!"'

Jeffrey, an exhibiting photographer, visual artist and graphic designer, kept the battered lion for two decades before it officially became the founding member of his very first collection – of animal figure misfits. A small rubber cow was another early addition to the collection. It was also severely disabled, with a twisted right foot and a punctured and patched stomach, and could no longer stand properly. Later a tiny handmade albino elephant with no ears joined the motley crew, along with an extended family of hand-carved wooden horses, deer, pigs, dogs and donkeys. To Jeffrey, the damaged and quirky animals 'have left the world of toys behind and

are real in the world as unique and serious objects even if sometimes playful in their countenance'.

Jeffrey's collections decorate almost every wall and surface of the home he shares in the Catskills with his partner, Rebecca Purcell. They are also integral to his art practice. Brushes are his most substantial collection. His first brush was purchased from the same flea market where he had found the lion a year or two earlier. 'I was into fibre arts at the time and the brush was sculptural, utilitarian and was also like a weaving – a fibre artwork.' Its curvilinear, flowing shape 'spoke to this idea of natural forms and movement being incorporated into design and art'. It also appeared to fuse elements of Art Nouveau design with strong Asian aesthetic influences. 'Whenever I do an installation of brushes, I almost always hang this brush first and then place all the others relative to it. I try to honour it as the originator of the collection, even though when I bought it I didn't know it was the beginning of a collection. Plus, it is the most asymmetrical brush I own, so it is difficult to fit into a grid once it is started!' Whenever he moves to a new place, Jeffrey brings in this brush first, along with a large bundle of *Ailanthus altissima* (tree of heaven) sticks as a kind of ritualistic claiming and welcoming. 'Both objects speak of home and transition to me.'

Many of the other brushes in his collection are small by comparison, including one with a wooden handle carved into the shape of a dog's head. The perfectly aligned natural bristles make it look as though the dog is elegantly dressed in a long brown skirt. There are also hairbrushes, toothbrushes, shoe polish brushes, shaving brushes, nailbrushes, paintbrushes and back scrubbers. Dozens of the brushes cover the wall of the dining room. Others are arranged on small shelves around the house.

For Jeffrey, the brushes are 'symbols of individuality in the context of sameness and the homogenised consumer culture that we live in. In their most simplistic way, they're designed to order and organise your world, most often by moving what is often natural dirt on your floor or things from the outside world coming in. So brooms and brushes were created to try to exert some kind of control on that interaction.' He is attracted to older brushes because they express a sense of history, both of their own functional lives and of lives of the people who have used them. Some are broken, such as a salvaged brush fragment from a New York City street sweeping truck. 'They rotate these big disks of metal spines and bristles, but one broke off. It still feels like a brush, but it's now a sculpture because it has lost its context.'

His other collections include paint-by-number animals, which cover the wall of one of the guest bedrooms; rulers and other measuring devices; metal animals; photographs damaged through darkroom or photographer error; snapshots of Christmas trees; rocks; and miniature animal trophy heads. He also has a collection of balls that he found over approximately five years in a Hudson River eddy under the George Washington Bridge in Manhattan. One of his most extensive collections is of postcards. He has more than 15,000 of them covering a range of nature topics like dogs, bears, alligators, birds and horses.

Signs, mostly vintage or handpainted, form another collection and are displayed individually or in clusters in incongruous contexts around the house and property to provide amusement. A sign declaring 'Men Working in Trees' hangs on a brick wall in the sitting room. A small, rustic 'Hello I'm Johnny Cash' sign is installed in front of a tree near the creek that runs through their property. 'Rib Roast 15¢' is attached to a wall on the upstairs landing, near a shelf displaying beaver skulls, and a sign urging readers to 'Look for Dog' is found inside the back door, with only decidedly unmenacing stuffed dogs and dog figurines in sight.

For Jeffrey, the Catskills house only became a home when he surrounded himself with these objects. 'I think anywhere I end up being, I want a collective sensibility of the things that I own around me … if I am in a hotel room for more than a day, it'll start having a collection.' The home,

which they call Stump House, provides the perfect opportunity for the objects to 'have a resting place'.

Jeffrey and Rebecca began renting the home in 1994, before eventually buying it about ten years later. They divide their time between the home and their apartment in New York, and have studio spaces in both. The white 19th-century Catskills farmhouse features original wainscot walls and beadboard ceilings in many of the rooms. It is nestled on five-and-a-half acres of land in an area famous for its kaleidoscopic showcase of ever-changing seasonal colours.

While Jeffrey's work is closely connected to nature, he is also fascinated by the intersection between manufactured objects and natural forms. Living between the Catskills and New York exposes him to both. 'I have always been attracted to manmade things that are being broken down by nature, so they become a bridge – they express two different things. You still understand what they were, but you also start to sense that they are vulnerable and that they're part of the natural process.'

Jeffrey sees himself not as a maker but someone who frames ideas and poses visual questions through his assembly of objects, or their isolation, or an unexpected change in environment. 'I'm not a painter or a sculptor in the classical sense, but I see relationships between things that have meaning outside their immediate assigned purpose.'

Similarly, he is interested in how Western society uses Cartesian measurements and grids to exert some control over the natural world. 'Nature is just this amorphous, borderless thing and then for us to have possession of it, we project onto it, often with right-angle sensibilities.' Whether it is fences dividing land or frames creating a viewpoint around an artwork, it is the questions around defining and cropping that interest Jeffrey. 'They lead me to work a lot with traditional frames as part of the artwork itself, often framing earth,

For Jeffrey … brushes are 'symbols of individuality in the context of sameness and the homogenised consumer culture that we live in.'

grass, fur and things that were kind of archetypes of nature.'

Jeffrey's late father was an astrophysicist and head of the Department of Physics at North Carolina State University. He was a man of few words, although he shared some key ideas with his two sons. While Jeffrey's language wasn't maths and his aptitude wasn't for physics or calculus, he 'gained an understanding that there are different languages of knowing nature. Abstraction of math, science, or physics creates a language of symbols and numbers to understand very real things that we have all experienced or thought about in an empirical way.'

It was Jeffrey's older brother, Steve, who showed him how to follow a creative path. The brothers' shared interest in collecting and animals began in childhood. Jeffrey covered the sloping ceiling of his bedroom with animal images from books and magazines to create a giant collage of the animal kingdom. Steve had pet lizards, spiders and turtles and collected rocks and fossils. He also had an interest in astronomy and liked to blow things up in a small chemistry lab.

... He is interested in how Western society uses Cartesian measurements and grids to exert some control over the natural world.

Steve knew from an early age that he wanted to be a graphic designer. When he started studying at the School of Design at North Carolina State University, he told Jeffrey it was a good place for de-education. Jeffrey remembers his advice vividly. 'He explained that we go through a process from kindergarten through high school of a certain kind of programmatic learning, and that to be a designer–artist, you have to unlearn some of that so that you can see a way of being creative in terms of problem-solving or seeing the world. His point was that, no matter what you do, it will help you find your own way of seeing the world, of trying to break down the way it works, how you see it and how to problem-solve within it.'

The first time Jeffrey visited his brother on campus, he went to a class in the Fundamental Design Department that was held in a cavernous room with high ceilings. The teacher had asked the students to build an environment and live in it for three days. 'There were freestanding treehouse structures in a classroom, and there were people sleeping in them.' It was open twenty-four hours a day, so there was always something going on. 'I thought, "Oh, this is really good, this is different," and so that drew me in.'

Jeffrey chose to study at The Cooper Union in New York City. He has gone on to establish himself as a unique voice in the world of book design, designing and editing *David Sedaris Diaries: A Visual Compendium* (2017). You can also see the influence of his design training in the visual organisation of his art-based installations, which are anchored in structure and compositional strength. Jeffrey has exhibited his work in the USA and Europe and is often involved in collaborative projects, such as with J Morgan Puett in her exhibition space, The Mildred Complex(ity), in the tiny town of Narrowsburg in New York.

Whether designing books, assembling rocks into a box to consider in a new way, or exploring flea markets and forests for objects that speak to him, Jeffrey has a unique and authentic viewpoint. His collections-based projects have meaning beyond the decorative. He believes that collecting 'helps give you identity. It's a way of measuring and placing yourself in the world, finding and identifying things that are specific and personal to you.' Walking through the Catskills house feels a little like visiting pockets of Jeffrey's mind. With each collection, you see a little more of the artist's character, and why he calls this place home. ◆

ROBERT BAINES

The Art of the Goldsmith

As a young boy, Dr Robert Baines helped in his father's upholstery and French polishing workshop in Greensborough, near Melbourne, Australia. More than sixty years later, his recollections of the layout and details of the workshop are vivid, as are his memories of working alongside his father.

Surrounded by the wooden skeletons of chairs, couches and settees, all awaiting their new clothes, Robert learnt the basic principles of design, technique and self-discipline. His father taught him to remove old tacks, webbing and fabric from the furniture using a mallet and chisel. Breathing air thick with the scent of natural gelatinous glue heating in a tin pot, Robert helped strip the furniture back to its simple, bare frame. 'That was my first experience of a real workshop.'

The idyllic relationship between a master craftsman and his very young apprentice was soon shattered. In 1957, when Robert was only eight years old, his father died suddenly in the night. 'His death was a big, big shock. I woke up and I could hear my mother running around the house and screaming.' The workshop was closed, the building was rented out, and his father's tools were packed away. But the lessons were not forgotten. Robert continued to work with his hands, improvising with materials like matchsticks, toilet rolls, cotton wool and papier-mâché. Later, while doing classes in metalwork at secondary school, he decided to become a goldsmith. He reclaimed his father's tools and they began a second life in his hands.

Robert's trajectory from young assistant in his father's workshop to internationally renowned goldsmith and scholar has been gradual and focused, yet he is virtually unknown to the Australian public. Over the course of his distinguished career, he has been honoured with many scholarships and fellowships that have enabled him to study the collections and work with staff at some of the world's most prestigious art institutions. His work is held in major public and private collections around the world including London's Victoria and Albert Museum, the Metropolitan Museum of Art in New York, and the National Gallery of Australia.

Although he enjoys an international standing, he consciously lives a quiet and simple life. Work, home and family are at the centre, and all other distractions are kept to a minimum. 'I like the isolation. It's a personal world, it's not overstated. There are no interventions from traffic lights, and sirens, and busyness. There's a quietness here in the countryside.'

Unsurprisingly, his philosophy as a goldsmith has been built on the same basic principles he learnt in his father's workshop, where a deep respect and reverence was given to the preparation of an object's frame. 'The thing that really intrigued me was the preparatory work – you get back to the frame – you *start* with the frame. There was a lot of stitching and preliminary work. First, attaching the webbing to the frame, which holds the springs, and stitching the springs on. Then you put the cover over, then the veneer, then the diamond buttoning. My father had these long needles that he used to thread through the webbing, the horsehair and coconut fibre that was part of the padding. I still have the needles at home.'

As a goldsmith, he now works with wire frames upon which he builds a web of delicate filaments. They form a network of interconnecting metal threads that mimic structural patterns found in the natural world. His creations can be appreciated both as exquisite sculptural artefacts and as jewellery. For Robert, they are 'personal objects that have meaning' and his pursuit of new forms and structures is a continual process. In a short piece titled *The Crinkle and Crankle of Wire* he details the thinking that underpins his work: 'Rhythm is wire and space, wire is the line, line measures space, line captures space, line is the meter of poetry, line is the poetry of matter, space is the matter of poetry, does poetry matter? Wire networks comprise planar surfaces of variable patterning, with a repetition of line and space. This creates a *poësis* (poetics of making).'

The same principles of structure and design have, perhaps unwittingly, been applied to the layout of the property where Robert lives with his wife, Pearl, and the youngest of their three adult sons, Jack. Robert describes the home and grounds, set on five acres on the rural outskirts of Melbourne, as being an 'archaeology of my family's life'.

The home's interiors bear no relationship or resemblance to Robert's work, except for the many stained-glass windows that he and Pearl made to decorate the house. Its original architectural style is virtually undetectable as a result of the multiple additions, add-ons, renovations and prior uses. In the 1890s it was used as a tea-house, providing refreshments for the tennis courts that used to operate opposite the house, on the other side of a dirt track. In later years, a midwife used the house as the local birthing centre.

Robert's trajectory from young assistant in his father's workshop to internationally renowned goldsmith and scholar has been gradual and focused ...

The site is carved up by a series of pathways that divide and capture the space. 'Pathways are curious, each has its own significance and importance.' There is the path past the children's old cubby house, the path from the shed up to the driveway that is framed with white quartz, and the little dirt path around the dam to the tiny hut that Robert built as a shrine to his mother. He cut the latest path through thick bamboo with the help of his grandsons. 'I like entering the density and darkness – there is a spectacle in it. Sometimes I stand in there and I watch the birds down on the dam. I like travelling through all this vegetation in semi-darkness, and then there is an openness, a little vista at the end.'

One of the most important paths on the property leads from the house to the studio. Robert attributes great meaning to walking that pathway:

leaving the house, which is full of all the eclectic paraphernalia and distractions of family life, and approaching his studio. The pathway provides 'a process of transition, of arriving at the studio for the day. It's not confused by domestic or family things – it's an isolation … a separation.' For some time after he built his studio, Robert wouldn't even allow his dog inside. But, over time, he has softened and his current dog, Rufus, is a regular fixture of the space. Rufus's mop of cream fur is easy to spot as he rests on the floor.

In contrast to the home, Robert's studio was designed and built with a singular, uncompromising focus. 'The studio and home are completely different polemics. I don't like the overlap and confusion of having a studio and home together.' His studio was not designed to impress, or even interest, others. It had to satisfy Robert's practical and creative needs and reflect his deeply spiritual nature. He built the studio in 1975 with the help of a family friend, the late Ted Rock, who became a father figure to Robert after his father's death. Robert remembers Ted as 'an intellectual builder – some sort of scriptural carpenter'.

The design of the studio is not reflective of any current architectural trend or style. It was influenced by a treatise written in the Middle Ages by Theophilus Presbyter, a Benedictine monk and metalworker. The three-volume work includes *The Art of the Metalworker*, which provides practical directives for artists working with metal. Robert followed many of Presbyter's detailed guidelines when he was designing and setting up his studio. The text explains that the goldsmith should sit at a bench at a north-facing window, so there is no direct sunlight coming in. Transposing Presbyter's northern hemisphere design to a southern hemisphere model, Robert positioned his workbenches facing south. He built a bank of windows that run almost the whole length of the wall, salvaging wood for the window frames from nearby wrecking yards.

The resulting light that fills the space is what photographers call open shade – a luminous shade without sharp contrasts. It is a favourite of gold and silversmiths, who work with flames to soften the metal. 'If you have direct sunlight, you can't see the flame. The flame is intimately connected to the goldsmith. I blow air into the fire and my breath changes the size of the flame. It can be a needle flame, a pencil flame, or a bushy brush flame, all within an instant – and that's just with the control of the breath. So, to see the flame is critical.'

The Art of the Metalworker also resonated with Robert's deep need to understand the history of his craft, and the personal context that understanding provides. 'What is really significant about this text is this is the first metal treatise known. For three millennia of ancient pre-Christian goldsmithing there is no text, no explanation. Then suddenly there is this – a whole different thinking process: how you venerate the craft, how you have responsibilities. There is a beautiful integrity in that code of behaviour for the goldsmith. As a young goldsmith, this resonated with me.'

Each chapter in the treatise is dedicated to a different subject and espouses a combination of practical information that is as relevant to metalwork artists today as it was more than 900 years ago. 'I like to make small precious objects – personal objects that are imbued with meaning, but I am engaging in strategies of working that come from this historical goldsmith. It's like a contemporary pianist who sits down and plays a historical piece. There is this opportunity to engage in something that takes you out of this world, and into another world. But it's got values and conditions that resonate with the human experience. It abounds in meaning.'

The philosophy behind the design of Robert's studio doesn't stop there. He applied spiritual concepts to the layout, choosing height, width and depth dimensions in multiples of three to make a Trinitarian statement. He also uses multiples of three in his creative work, such as in the preparation of *The Entropy of Red – Trumpet* (1995), which can be found in the collection of the Victoria and Albert Museum. 'In fine wire work you have to tie pieces together and I count in multiples of three. It's a type of worship. Presbyter talks about … a *worthyship* in this work, and he links worthyship with worship. It's a belief system. It's imbued and embedded with the making.'

While the studio itself is not particularly photogenic, that is not its purpose. A close-up lens is needed to fully appreciate the beauty of the space. It is a hidden sea of texture, tone and form. Among the dozens of tools lining the studio's main room is a large wooden mallet that belonged to Robert's father. Robert remembers using it in his father's workshop when he was a boy. In another homage to his history, he built a long, thin shelf at the far end of the studio to display a family of plaster moulds that were saved from the days when his parents worked together in the Fowlers pottery factory in the 1940s.

Surrounded by these memories, and using the tools his father used before him, Robert creates artefacts and original jewellery objects. These precious little revelations, built around intricate miniature frames of wire, are the continuation of the legacy of a master craftsman. ◆

One of the most important paths on the property leads from the house to the studio. Robert attributes great meaning to walking that pathway.

ANNABELLE ADIE

A Little Corner of Paris

What does 'home' mean for someone whose formative years were often disrupted by change? Is it idealised, or diminished, or is the traditional concept of home replaced by an adaptable 'interior' home, lived within the mind and body itself, undefined by walls and geography? Artist Annabelle Adie's early years gave rise to opposing impulses – a strong desire for a stable home base, and also a restless spirit. 'Home is everywhere I go, in a way. I'm at home everywhere, and nowhere.'

When Annabelle was eight years old, her Scottish father separated from her French–English mother and left the family in London to live in Australia with his new wife. In the unsettling wake of her father's departure, Annabelle relocated to Paris with her mother, leaving three older siblings behind in English boarding schools. Annabelle tried a number of different schools in France before eventually settling into the École Internationale Bilingue, which she recalls was 'full of misfits like me – which was nice'.

A few years later, Annabelle was sent back across the English Channel to board at West Heath Girls School in Kent. 'I had become the little French girl … it took me a year to become someone who people would dare come near.' Eventually she was accepted into the small student community that included children from high-profile families.

Annabelle spent her school holidays in Paris or the south of France, depending on the time of year. 'I spent my life ping-ponging from France to the UK, and then added Italy to my list in my teens.' Although her home life was always changing, she was 'very aware of environment, right from the beginning'. As a young girl, she was

'always into the idea of a context and creating an environment'. Her favourite pastime was creating elaborate miniature homes for her dolls, including furniture and little accessories, using materials like cardboard, paint, plastic and fabric.

After completing tertiary studies at ESAG Penninghen art school in Paris, and a year at the Accademia delle Belle Arte in Rome, Annabelle's creative confidence had grown, and so had her desire to create a home of her own. In her mid-twenties, she bought an apartment in an 1820s building in Montmartre, Paris. It has now been her home address for more than three decades.

The apartment is an expression of her creativity – she calls it her 'antidepressant' – which is essential to her emotional wellbeing. 'I have a conscious awareness that I am fighting depression every single minute of my life … I have found my creative work is one of the best ways to harness it.'

Annabelle's unique visual lexicon speaks in fabric, light, colour and clay. She applies these elements to a myriad of uses – commercial and artistic, personal and public. Sometimes the colours that she chooses for her home, her clothes, her artwork and even her lipstick seem so particular, so distinct, that she almost owns them. It's as though she has developed a sixth sense, which she uses to create a conversation in colour.

She admits to being abnormally colour-sensitive and describes certain colours in terms of need. In one of the smallest rooms in her home, a tiny library where she has created ceramic boxes which hang from the wall to house books, she spoke of a growing need to paint the walls green. Not just any green, but a very particular shade. 'It does not fall into any obvious category of greens: it's not olive, or moss, or grass, or pea.'

Perhaps her compulsion to create such a specific hue can be explained by her growing reconnection with Scotland, the land of her paternal ancestors. The Scottish landscape and her family tartan are awash with various shades of green that she now embraces and uses to dress her home and herself. 'Rediscovering my roots in Scotland has been wonderful and surprising to me ... discovering a kindred spirit in the character of the Scots – their humour and eccentricity and the sheer beauty of the colours and landscapes – has been a fabulous revelation.'

She occasionally uses very strong, even fluorescent, colour like exclamation points or question marks. However, when it comes to her ceramics, she works at the other extreme, restricting the palette to white clay with a white glaze, or russet clay painted in white slip and glaze. Again, she describes her approach in terms of need: 'a need for purity and simplicity, in contrast with all the other effervescence of colour and texture'. The resulting sculptural works give a feeling of utter tranquillity. Feelings have been distilled and transformed through the clay into an exquisite world of creative symbols that imbue her home with a unique visual signature.

Every wall in every room of her apartment showcases her ability to work with paint, clay, wire and paper. Rope, wool, velvet, linen, cotton and silk (often hand-dyed) are also favoured materials. She mixes her own paints from pigments, then marks each wall with symbols, shapes and seemingly random abstract patches. The wall paintings create the backdrop for her ceramic and fabric works that hang in little clusters throughout the apartment.

Annabelle buys her colour pigments from Zecchi art supplies in Florence, and adds a watercolour, acrylic or oil base. She stores the pigments in large glass jars with the original labels stuck to the front: Terra di Sienna, Cobalto Chiaro, Ocra Gialla and Nero Fumo. Zecchi is famous for finding and reviving ancient paint recipes used by master Italian artists of the Renaissance and pre-Renaissance eras. Their pigments include ground earth, saffron, Afghan lapis, carbon, vegetable extracts and dried squid ink powder. 'They are the exact palette of colours used in all the wonderful Giotto frescoes, and also reproduce

all the beautiful colours of the buildings in Italy.' The Italian colour palette has inspired her more than any other. 'I think all those palazzos are magnificent ... that particular ability the Italians have of combining the decrepit and the really sumptuous.'

She used this Italian colour palette to paint the ceiling plaster mouldings in the open-plan sitting room and the dining room. After buying the apartment in 1986, it was a few years before she had the courage to get up high enough on a ladder to paint the decorative moulding. Until then, she had reluctantly lived with the paintwork that was there when she purchased the apartment. 'All the mouldings were painted as though they were fake wood – they were dark brown and really, really ugly and oppressive. It looked like some nasty pub.' She was finally motivated to act by the discovery of three Zecchi colours in the same hues that had captured her attention on ceiling plasterwork in a Florentine palazzo. 'That inspired me, and I just did it.'

In another room, Annabelle has created a studio space that is a wash of whites, pale dusty pinks, yellows and creams. Fabric cuttings in velvets, silk, linen and cotton sit in piles around the room, and works in progress are organised along two work tables and a long shelf. Canvas cuttings, which have been painted in muted tertiary tones, sit in small stacks alongside others painted in various shades of matt white. Adjacent to the studio is a heavy-duty workshop where all the messy paint mixing takes place. Paint-stained aprons hang in the corner, brushes of all widths sit in pots and a large sink and drying area line one wall of the room.

A third work room is set up as an office space, which Annabelle shares with her Italian husband, architect Ernesto Buttafoco. As well as the necessary desks and computers, there is a white linen couch and a fireplace framed by a black marble mantelpiece. A flock of Annabelle's ceramic works hang quietly on the wall.

The Scottish landscape and her family tartan are awash with various shades of green that she now embraces ...

Colour, light and texture also define the master bedroom. With a small balcony and large French windows, the room looks down on a bustling Montmartre intersection. In the centre of the bedroom floor, a large circular parquetry feature catches the sun. The walls display ceramic works and other treasures, including a selection of faded cardboard filing folders, framed for their colours.

Every summer, as Paris heats to melting point, Annabelle escapes for several months to her husband's family home on the Italian coast in the Marche that is 'literally far from anything'. She uses this time to work on her ceramics, glazing and firing them before bringing them back to Paris. Each year, as winter closes in on France, Annabelle transforms her apartment into an installation of the new work, and hosts a party to share it with friends.

Annabelle is adept at transforming, reinventing and adapting, and much of her ceramic work reflects on these changing states. The physical process of working with clay also appeals to her fascination with material metamorphosis. 'One of the things that attracted me to ceramics was the opportunity to participate in a process of extreme transformation usually only available in a lab. From a soft or liquid "natural" matter, the clay – modelled, dried, then fired until the temperature reaches 1000 °C – becomes incandescent then hardens as it cools. On opening the kiln, you discover a completely new material, irreversibly transformed … there is always a margin of unpredictable variables, which give an essence of miracle or, occasionally, disaster!'

Test tubes and the accoutrements of chemistry and biology labs also appeal to her interest in changing states. She has created little families of ceramic test tubes that hang from vivid coloured rope on the wall. Other frequently explored visual symbols are keys and keyholes. Aside from her love of their simple shapes, they suggest 'unlocking and opening another space … the transition from one room to another'.

Instead of denying life's wounding experiences or repressing ugliness, she explores them and finds beauty in imperfection. 'It's like therapy for me.' Her giant-sized ceramic chains, for example, are 'not linked to constriction and imprisonment. It's much more a question of the links connecting and creating a strength, of joining two things – very much the opposite of something constrictive or torturous.'

This ability to reimagine concepts and rethink the meaning of everyday objects is part of what enables Annabelle to create such a distinctive home. The interiors are lyrical and playful, and her home is so warm and inviting that the challenges of her formative years are seemingly erased. This is someone who has the talent and determination to channel loss and dislocation into a tactile visual language that not only attracts like-minded people, but shows them, through art and beauty, a way to feel at home in the world. ◆

139

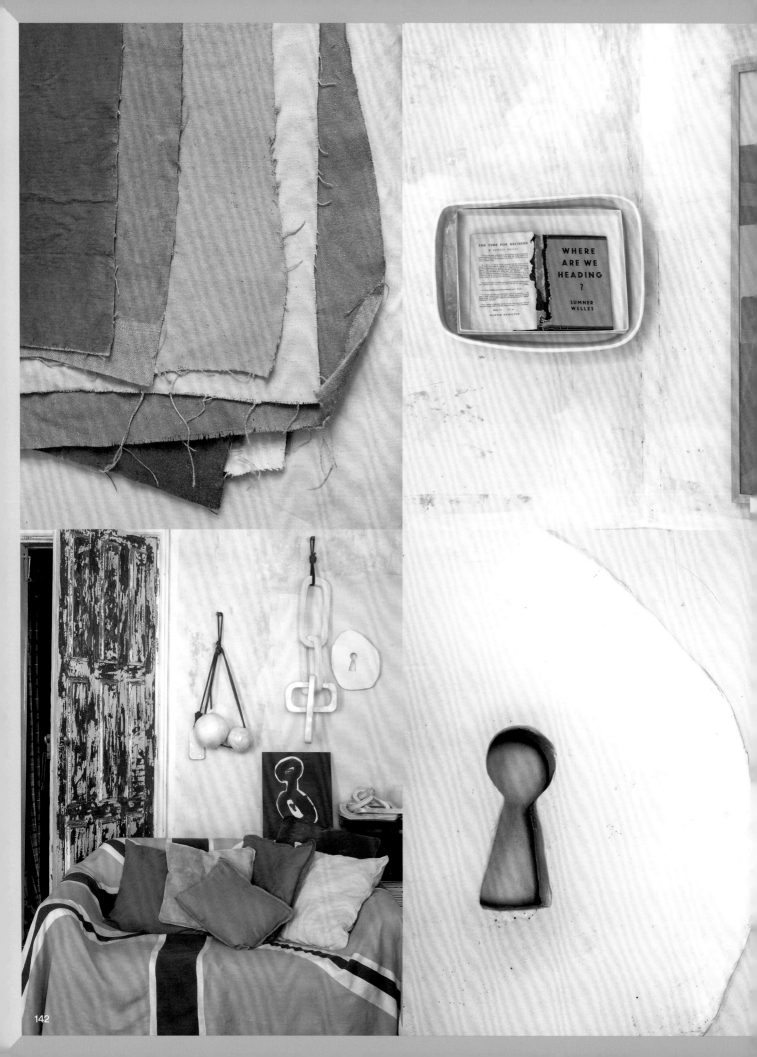

WHERE
ARE WE
HEADING
?

SUMNER
WELLES

THE TIME FOR DECISION

NATHALIE LÉTÉ

An Enchanted Universe

Artist Nathalie Lété's private realm in Paris is like a fantasy land, one large step removed from reality. It is a world she shares with her husband, artist Thomas Fougeirol, their two children Angèle and Oskar, Coco the canary, their dachshund Spike, and a host of imaginary friends. As an only child growing up in a household with parents who were often unhappy and frequently absent, she dreamed of living in a wonderful environment. From a very early age, she went about creating it. 'I didn't like my home when I was a kid. I wanted to be surrounded with beautiful and colourful things and create harmony.'

The process was cathartic. She started on a small scale, making toys for herself, decorating her bedroom and painting constantly. 'I was always creating stories with my toys – they were like my friends, my family.' As soon as she had money of her own, she purchased some old furniture at a flea market and covered it with painted decorations. She was captivated by Chinese and German folk stories (her father was Chinese and her mother German), and the plots of classic fairy tales fuelled her imagination.

When she was eighteen, she went to see an astrologer who predicted she would become a successful artist whose work would be connected with childhood. The prediction gave her the confidence to abandon the idea of becoming a flight attendant and become an artist instead. She established a creative business with her former boyfriend under the name Mathias et Nathalie, and for ten years they created cardboard sculptures for a host of clients around the world.

Later, she met Thomas at the Beaux Arts de Paris and they married and had their first child. With Mathias et Nathalie now over, Nathalie realised that she needed to find her own creative voice. This was a slow and difficult process after a decade of collaborative work. After grappling with it for some time, unable to work or see a way forward, she turned to a subject that was close to her heart.

One day, while her daughter Angèle slept in her cot, Nathalie did a painting of a toy she remembered playing with when she was young. It was a turning point. She subsequently tapped into a rich undercurrent of childhood themes and slowly her creative confidence was restored. In many ways, the themes and materials she works with have changed very little from when she was a child. Her favourite subjects are still animals, flowers, vintage toys, fairy tales and folk art, and her preferred mediums include ceramics, embroidery, textiles and paint. She is happy in her own company and sometimes prefers the companionship of her stuffed animals and handmade dolls to people. While she tends to keep to herself and her immediate family, she loves the idea that her creations are sent around the world and give people joy.

After the birth of their second child, Nathalie and Thomas realised they needed more living and work space. They purchased a home in Ivry-sur-Seine, on the outskirts of Paris. Their two-storey townhouse is inside a vast converted factory where many of the wrought-iron frames for the Eiffel Tower were built in the 1880s. Evidence of the building's impressive history abounds, although much of it is now hidden among climbing plants and abundant gardens. Massive pulley systems, which once carried some of the 18,000 pieces of metal required to build Paris's most famous monument, create an imposing overhead structure of handsome impotence. Pathways are wide, ceilings are high and the light that spills through oversized wood-framed windows is soft and broad.

Along with the townhouse, they were also able to secure two studios inside the same complex. The three-minute walk between their home and studios allows them to focus almost completely on work and family. Nathalie's quiet studio is on the ground floor, with an entrance through a small, verdant garden. Thomas has his studio on the floor above, with a separate entrance via an external staircase.

An oversized papier-mâché bunny dressed in a suit and tie presides over the main room of Nathalie's workspace. Toy poodles, piggies and a miniature wooden Pinocchio sit in jumbled harmony with ceramic eyeballs, snails and forest mushrooms. A vase in the form of a sleeping woman's head sits on a small, dark box next to a cabinet stuffed full of fabrics that Nathalie has designed. Lamp bases shaped like rabbits and trees sit under lampshades painted with butterflies, owls, foxes and birds.

Fairy tales continue to inspire her work and she frequently paints scenes from *Little Red Riding Hood*, with its naive protagonist under threat from the wolf lurking nearby. 'Fairy tales always have their dark sides.' *Alice's Adventures in Wonderland* and *Hansel and Gretel* are also favourites and her paintings of their stories are printed on tables, trays, ceramics, scarves and bags. Sometimes Nathalie digresses from the original plots, placing the main characters into new scenarios. In one image, Little Red Riding Hood is not walking along a forest path to visit her ill grandmother, or standing by the bedside of a wolf in a bonnet, but is found at a flea market where a stand is selling vinyl records by Nina Simone for twenty cents each.

Although Nathalie learnt not to rely on people during childhood, her connection with nature was strengthened. Many of her favourite subjects are inspired by her relationship with the natural world. Almost every weekend she walks in the nearby Bois de Vincennes, which was converted from a royal hunting preserve into the largest park in Paris by Napoleon III in the mid-1800s. The garden is home to 400 varieties of fruit trees, 650 varieties of iris and 300 varieties of lilac.

The grounds include four lakes and Château de Vincennes, which was home to many generations of French royalty. The Bois de Vincennes is a tonic for Nathalie, and its plants and resident birds often appear in her work. When she is working in her studio, she plays a soundscape of birdcalls that is similar to the ones she hears in the park, and her pet canary responds to their chatter from his cage.

In addition to her family home and studio in Ivry-sur-Seine, Nathalie also has a tiny apartment in central Paris. Based in the 2nd arrondissement, formerly a garment district, the single-room, 124-square-metre studio was once part of a button factory. When she found it, it had been gutted and stripped to its bare bones: an empty room with a large bank of windows that looked down on the narrow street below. Determined to create a private sanctuary, Nathalie installed a nest-like bed that seems to float above the floor – it is a hybrid between a miniature caravan and a private sleeping carriage inside a train. One entire wall is covered in her handpainted tiles featuring owls, ravens, flowers and ferns, and the tiny kitchen is full of objects she has designed, including teapots, milk jugs, bowls, plates, trays and cups. Handmade porcelain light fittings in the shapes of flowers hang from the ceilings, and wooden boards painted in the softest of mossy greens cover the floor. Like a miniature Bloomsbury-style home in the middle of Paris, every surface is painted and every corner is full of Nathalie's creations.

Nathalie is an artist enveloped in a wonderful dreamscape of flowers, animals and toys. Her artwork and lyrical vision of the world have helped her break a cycle of unhappiness that often travels down through generations. She has achieved her long-held dream of living in a beautiful and loving home and her work has given joy to countless people around the world. ◆

> The Bois de Vincennes is a tonic for Nathalie, and its plants and resident birds often appear in her work.

GAVIN BROWN AND PETER CURNOW

His and His Apartments

Gavin Brown and Peter Curnow live side-by-side in neighbouring apartments on the first floor of a 1920s Spanish Mission building in St Kilda, a bayside suburb in Melbourne, Australia. Entering their homes feels like stepping into a combined travel journal, visual diary and art installation. The apartments are separated by a small external landing, which is decorated with a dozen Moroccan pendant lamps, Buddhist sculptures and a collection of cacti and yucca plants.

Their friends are accustomed to starting an evening with aperitifs and hors d'oeuvres in Gavin's sitting room, followed by a five-second walk to Peter's place where the table is set for dinner. In the warmer months, drinks are often served after dinner on the landing to the rustle of palm leaves and the light scent of pastries from the many Polish cake shops nearby.

'Everyone laughed when we told them Peter was buying the flat next door. They said, "Why don't you just buy a house together?" But now everyone is saying "That's the smartest thing anyone's ever done!"'

Peter adds, 'We love the idea of maintaining two distinct homes that can become one at will.'

Gavin is a painter and printmaker, and occasional textile and interior designer. 'I hope that I will draw my last breath with a brush or pencil in my hand.' His textile designs have been collected by the Powerhouse Museum in Sydney, the National Gallery of Victoria in Melbourne, and Victoria and Albert Museum in London, among others. In the 1990s he ran nightclubs where, in an extension of his art practice, he would often perform in drag, making all of his own outfits. 'I see everything as an artist, so if I am creating an interior, or creating food, or creating a painting, it comes from the same place.'

Gavin's decorating style is influenced by his earliest childhood memories. 'Growing up I had three great aunts, who were very elderly Edwardian ladies and all lived together. They had a Victorian house with a parlour and all the interiors were very dark, and very intense, with heavy antique furniture and palms.' Gavin's sitting room has a similar atmosphere, which he has created using a riotous mix of antiques and contemporary objects and layers of colour and texture in each room, 'like a large still life with a modern baroque sensibility'.

The eclectic interior of his apartment includes a life-size wooden goat from India with detachable testicles that stands under the mantelpiece, cushions Peter made from antique textiles purchased in Istanbul, a wooden carving of Quan Yin (the Buddhist bodhisattva known as the Goddess of Mercy), a bunch of hand-carved Japanese altar flowers, 18th-century gold candlesticks from France and Portugal, and a white urn with dancing cherubs framed in a fluorescent pink perspex box.

Sometimes Gavin buys an object on the spur of the moment, but he has also waited for years to acquire the right piece for a room. One of his longest waits was for an early-18th-century silver-gilded reliquary bust from Italy, which would have once carried a small bone or lock of hair in its niche. From the first time he saw it to the moment he purchased it, twenty years had passed. The piece now has a prominent place in his sitting room along with an evolving assortment of treasures from around the world. 'My home is my stage, my jewel box, my haven and my cabinet of curiosities. I get to edit my personal drama there.'

Many of the items and objects in Gavin's home represent important, longstanding friendships, like the large emerald-green sculpture by local artist William Eicholtz. Gavin acquired *Huysmans Cornucopia* (2007) in exchange for one of his paintings after the two held an exhibition together. Their friendship goes back to the early 1980s when they frequented Melbourne's club scene 'running around dressed up as New Romantics'.

Gavin's taste for creating an intoxicating atmosphere extends to his bedroom. 'Most people design a house for the day, but I design a house for the night, when I am there.' The room is dominated by a Chinese opium bed and tassels hang from its carved wooden frame. Bejewelled Indian wedding statues stand on either side of the window and a painting of Saint Teresa of Ávila in the last agonising throes of death hangs on the red lacquered wall.

By day, Gavin works in his studio, which is just a short walk from home in an old knitting mill factory that has been converted into twenty artists' spaces. In contrast to the dark mystery and soiree-friendly furnishings and fabrics of his apartment, the studio is full of light that streams through oversized windows. Clippings, drawings and photographs cover the walls and door in an evolving collage of ideas and influences. Images of tattooed faces are pinned alongside skulls with alarming gritted teeth, paper butterflies, Boy George and David Bowie.

Peter is a textile artist. His interest in making things with fabric also began in childhood, in the home of his grandmother who was a tailor. 'As a kid, I would get on the sewing machine. I have always had a passion for that. I would make clothes for my teddy bear. I remember making a sheepskin vest with a little braid trim.' His appreciation for fibres and textures began around the same time. 'I grew up on a farm that ran sheep for wool, which is such a beautiful fibre. I have always been attracted to fabric – to the fluidity of it. I am fascinated with the way it can be decorated, manipulated and crafted into almost limitless shapes and forms.'

As a young textile artist, Peter was the production controller in a boutique textile-printing firm in West London, working with clients such as textile designer Celia Birtwell and fashion designer Vivienne Westwood. 'I have known many strong and determined women who have influenced my work and career.' Now he divides his time between his home in Melbourne and wherever his inspiration or commissions take him. He inevitably returns from his trips abroad with fabric and materials that he uses to make lampshades, quilts, pillow covers and window furnishings, sometimes for clients but also to decorate his own apartment.

Peter's dining room is testament to his global quest for special treasures. A trip to Paris yielded two oxidised zinc lanterns and on his next visit he shipped home a mansard window frame. After inserting a convex mirror into the frame, he hung it between the two lanterns above the fireplace at the end of the dining table and surrounded it with a family of Fornasetti plates. To enhance the feel of 19th-century Europe, he made wallpaper from a photograph he had taken of ancient brickwork in Florence. 'You could go to a wallpaper pattern in a book and have it perfect but the whole idea is to see the character and all the cracks and the pattern that doesn't quite match up.'

Peter has an ability to place seemingly incongruous textures and objects next to each other in harmonious communion ...

Peter has an ability to place seemingly incongruous textures and objects next to each other in harmonious communion, a practice that began in his bedroom as a child. 'My father would not allow marking of the walls with holes or tape so I would arrange assorted "precious items" on my chest of drawers.' Hanging on one of his dining room walls is an image of a bright pink human skull with a full set of gleaming white teeth titled *Fang Shui* (2015) by his friend Chris Orr. It is flanked by a Qing dynasty southern Chinese fisherman's rain cape and a matching hat and vest, made from coconut fibre. Underneath, a big bowl of ostrich eggs is displayed on a red lacquered console from Kyoto. Next to that is a highly reflective bulbous glass sculpture by Australian artist Mark Douglass. 'I like to experiment with layering several diverse elements such as wood, metal and paper to create depth and perspective.' Objects from different eras are added to the fray, such as a white Rosenthal porcelain vase framed in a green perspex box that is displayed in front of a tall, hand-carved wooden figure of a bearded man wearing an eight-strand

Navajo coral necklace. Above the picture rail that encircles the room, Gavin has created a linocut frieze of black monkeys that are framed by printed flowers.

As in Gavin's apartment, each of Peter's rooms is like a chapter from a collection of short stories. They all have their own personality and narrative. As you enter the apartment through lattice screen doors, you meet the gaze of a woman in a sea of flowers. She is the subject of Gavin's painting *Wildflowers with Figure* (2013), which he gave Peter for his fiftieth birthday. They joke that Peter's apartment is the 'west wing storage unit', an evolving depository for Gavin's latest purchases. Peter often resists the process, which typically happens without his input, but he agrees it is also one of the best things about their relationship. 'I ask him, "What have you bought now?" and sometimes I refuse to have these things in my apartment – like that big carved head in the corner. I have never liked that! It lived in here for a while and then I said, "No, that's going!"'

While Peter was working on a project in Manila, Gavin secretly deposited a late-19th-century Irish table in his apartment. The table legs were carved in the shape of three dolphins with gold-accented gills, using the same techniques gypsies employed to decorate their horse-drawn vardo wagons. Gavin couldn't resist the purchase, despite not having the room to accommodate the piece in his own apartment. When Peter arrived home, he found the large round table had become the central feature of his dining room entrance area. 'It sort of dominates the room – how many more tables do I need? He just keeps shoving things in!'

While the two apartments often operate as one, they have their own distinct styles. The rich, shadowy tones of Gavin's apartment contrast with a lighter, brighter palette in Peter's. Peter's bedroom walls are painted a vivid tangerine hue that matches the flying cranes on two batik lampshades. A multicoloured patchwork quilt that covers the bed is made from fabric he silk-

screened when he was working for the artisanal textile house Vixen in Melbourne. Unlike the quilting traditions of North America, where cheap fabrics were often used and all the time and work were put into the hand-stitching of the quilt designs, Peter's quilt is made from valuable silks and velvets that have been painstakingly hand-printed then sewn with a machine.

The couple also share a love of travel, which they elevate to an art form and approach with the same theatrical joy and flair they use to decorate their apartments. They are drawn to a wildly diverse array of sites and experiences, from ancient ruins and historic palaces to bustling backstreet dives full of fabulous characters. From drag clubs in New York, to the Yuyuan Gardens in the Old City of Shanghai, to a Lebanese feast at Al Safadi in Abu Dhabi, every outing is approached with enthusiasm. When they are in Mandalay they always visit Zay Cho market, which sells everything from traditional velvet slippers to pickled tea leaves and fine handwoven textiles. In China, they head for the City God Temple of Shanghai for a heady mix of 'gods, gold and the sweet smoky scents of a thousand incense sticks', and in Turkey they shop at the Grand Bazaar.

Back home, their new acquisitions ignite a flurry of creative activity and rearranging of interiors. Peter explains, 'A newly discovered fabric or furniture item will usually trigger a minor reshuffle of the existing treasures. If my home looks a little bit like the Grand Bazaar in Istanbul, that's okay – bring it on, I say!' ◆

> As in Gavin's apartment, each of Peter's rooms is like a chapter from a collection of short stories.

REBECCA PURCELL

A Magical Corner of New York

Rebecca Purcell sits in the middle of her four-poster bed in the bedroom of the apartment she shares with her partner, Jeffrey Jenkins, in Washington Heights, New York. Her hair is done in two neat braids that sit on the lapels of her canvas jacket and a long grey fringe frames her face.

The very first time Rebecca saw a four-poster bed she was six years old. She lived in a simple suburban 1940s brick colonial-style house in Silver Spring, Maryland, on the outskirts of Washington DC. The décor of the family home, including the lighting and reproduction colonial furniture, did not appeal to Rebecca. She found the interiors 'actually quite disturbing'.

She spent a good deal of time at her friend Ginny's house. Ginny lived in a well-to-do area and her house was filled with Gothic, old-world antiques and heirlooms. 'This was the 70s, this was not what you saw in anybody else's house.' The master bedroom featured an immense bed with thick mahogany posts at each corner and a mattress that was so high off the ground that a small set of wooden steps was required to climb up. The bed was swathed in a huge feather down duvet, something that Rebecca had never seen before, and the pillows were dressed in fine linen covers. Children were forbidden from playing in the room, but sometimes the urge was too strong. When Ginny was otherwise occupied, Rebecca would sneak in and climb onto the bed. 'I would just sit there because I thought it was so phenomenal.'

Around that time, Rebecca began to build her own world in a hidden corner of the family home, far from the suburban ugliness that she felt infused many of the other rooms. 'Luckily my room was upstairs in the attic. At some point the space was finished off with proper walls but for several years it was an unfinished attic with piles of boxes everywhere. I made a narrow alley through the boxes that led to my bedroom, which was all the way up the far end, past all of the boxes and

debris, and *I loved it*.' Rebecca made a little pallet bed and used a sheet to make a canopy above it. 'It was just absolutely romantic and fabulous!'

Her eldest sibling, Debbie, created her bedroom in the basement. Rebecca recalls her sister 'spent her last year living at the house in a tiny cramped room at the back of our unfinished, cinder-block basement. With 60s bohemian flair [she was an intermittent follower of Indian mystic Rajneesh Bhagwan] and youthful angst, she turned the barrack-like room into a hippie den that smelled of sandalwood and mildew.'

Their mother was also going through a personal transformation, making a dramatic change from 1950s housewife to an earthy hippy who wore 'long skirts, Mexican shirts, and a scarf on her head'. In a clear rejection of the expectations of American women in the post-war period, she stopped maintaining a trim figure and quickly gained a lot of weight. 'I think she just wanted to bust out of that oppressive 50s mentality – she wanted out of all of it! I think she would have run away to California if she could have, but she would never have left us.'

When Rebecca left home she didn't go to college. She had already developed a solid confidence in her own creative interests and skills and wanted to start to work. 'I put everything in a car and left home, moving with a friend to Atlanta where I got a job in display in a department store.' She also started making garments and accessories by reconstructing thrift-store clothing. She put on fashion shows and became immersed in the punk new wave and clubbing scene in Atlanta before moving to New York in 1989.

In New York she began working at Charivari, an avant-garde clothing store with a cult following that championed the work of designers such as Helmut Lang and Issey Miyake. She was introduced to Paulette Cole, the creative director of ABC Carpet & Home, the influential carpet store that was about to become one of the most groundbreaking home furnishings stores in the world. Rebecca began working at ABC in 1990, just as homewares were introduced. 'It was just me as the display person and two stock guys in the beginning. I ended up as the display director with a staff of fifteen and tour buses stopping there.' Paulette was a creative visionary who wanted an environment that was more art installation than store display. 'I was given the space and free rein to create an immense, ongoing and ever-changing installation, expressing an ethos that I was later to realise had a significant cultural impact.' Every corner of the store was like a poetic film set. 'It was an immense phantasmagoria of objects, textiles and furniture, every area artfully arranged, with virtually no corner left empty.'

After seven years, she left the store to focus on her own personal art projects and her freelance work as an artist–stylist. Now her entire life is an art practice and includes everything she encounters: objects, home, wardrobe and aesthetics in general. She describes her style as Past–Present, which 'represents a cultural shift away from the pervasive and often destructive desire to impress which is fuelled by envy, wealth, status, power, and overt sexuality. Past–Present is highly diverse, cross-cultural, and is at times a swamp-like mingling of genres and styles.'

Many objects in the apartment represent a story of discovery or creation, with tremendous meaning infused in each piece.

The rooms of her apartment, as well as her installations, sets, still lifes and collages, are often created in layers. 'To me, layering and complexity is not useless clutter or mere decoration without content, nor is it chaotic or emotionally unstable.' She is attracted to objects and aesthetics that are 'incorporative: inclusive rather than exclusive, egalitarian rather than aspirational. An aesthetic expression honouring the string of ordinary lives that have left their impressions in weathered surfaces, dog-eared pages, worn wooden tool handles, and hand-sewn patches.'

Objects are chosen based on Rebecca's sensory reaction to them. Her blog documents much of her approach: 'The artist in me is continually searching for hints and clues among the forgotten, the time-worn, the discarded and the nostalgic, researching the evolution of consciousness and culture, looking for connections that may reveal a very different future – a kind of stepping backward to see forward. The stylist in me searches for nuance, looking for new relationships between objects, and creating physical association through placement. While not identical, they are similar and corresponding pursuits.'

Many objects in the apartment represent a story of discovery or creation, with tremendous meaning infused in each piece. For Rebecca, some objects have been permeated with a sacred element from their owners over time and collecting and preserving them is a way of honouring the many makers who have helped create beauty in our world.

Rebecca's collections include scraps of paper and fabric, sewing kits, miniature porcelain and ceramic birds, coin purses, hatpins, velvet boxes and picture frames, buttons, ribbons, antique or vintage dress collars and tiny found objects housed in a collection of vintage paper boxes tagged with gummed office labels. Sometimes she suffers from what she describes as 'acute moments of attraction' to an object that seems imbued with quasi-magical qualities. Describing a visit to an antique mall in upstate New York, she vividly recalls 'a tiny china figure took on totemic weight, a decal of salami became retro art of the highest calibre, a set of miniature Japanese lacquer bowls – sheer delight, and a blue glass owl seemed to be nothing less than a symbol of the deepest importance'.

Rebecca is a collector, but also a maker. One of her favourite activities is making fancy things from humble things: 'hi-end from low-end'. She starts with simple materials such as fabric offcuts, buttons, wire, paper, felt and pieces of plastic and gives them a new, and sometimes majestic, life. The practice of using readily available and cheap materials has the added benefit of ensuring she is always able to create regardless of her financial circumstances. Her apartment is full of examples of this type of work, including a long necklace made from paper, simple buttons and fabric scraps, and a collection of cardboard shapes covered in muted shades of worn velvet. Displayed in a cluster on a side table, they appear sculptural in their collective glory.

Certain early experiences continue to inspire Rebecca's work, including a clandestine viewing of David Lean's 1946 film, *Great Expectations*, which she watched in her sister's bedroom. 'Everything about the film was revelatory: the gentle, sincere, impoverished and abused boy whose life transforms through clothing and speech. The cinematic, sweeping grey vistas, the overgrown gardens, the neglected and creaking gate and Miss Havisham's house: all that wealth and grandeur buried in dust.' The film's final scene had a profound and lasting impact on Rebecca. 'When Pip wrenches the ancient decaying curtains from the windows, ripping away the old established order, ushering in a new, more egalitarian era – I felt that I too had been shown the light.'

In Rebecca's circle of friends, the simplest event can become performance art. For her birthday in 2001, J Morgan Puett and Mark Dion hosted a mushroom hunt party on their property, Mildred's Lane, in rural Pennsylvania. The guests were required to pack two costume changes: 'garb for the mushroom hunt, replete with mushrooming sticks, baskets and knives, followed by 50s-style attire for the cocktail soiree to follow'. As the troupe meandered through the property, they gathered mushrooms along with birthday gifts for Rebecca that were hidden in rock crevices and tucked into moss in the grass. Eventually they came to a clearing by the creek, where an assortment of wooden chairs was waiting. The gifts were unwrapped and they drank a bottle of champagne that had been nestling in a float, 'buoyed in the centre of the cooling stream'.

When I was photographing Rebecca's apartment, she appeared from time to time with a cluster of antique fabrics under her arm or a small suitcase or storage box full of treasures. 'These might interest you', or, 'You might like these'. Inside each container was a different collection. One was full of old pieces of torn paper, many of them in individual archival sleeves. Another had tiny scraps of frayed fabric in muted fuchsia and magenta shades. There was a delightful box of quirky, kitsch purses with little metallic clasps, beads, diamantes and zips, and miniature specimen boxes containing everything from animal teeth and fish bones to fake emerald rings and tiny metal keys.

Using Rebecca's collected treasures, I set up a series of still life shots on the floor in a soft patch of late winter light that was filtering through one of the sitting room windows. The colours, fabrics, shapes and textures began to speak to me as I arranged them in little families on top of one of the many fabrics. With each photograph, I felt further drawn into Rebecca's world, where everything has meaning, objects are not disposable, and the work of human hands from the past can in fact help us to navigate the uncertainty of the future. We finished the shoot with her portrait on her four-poster bed. The little girl is no longer forbidden from playing on the beautiful bed. She has grown up now and owns one herself. ◆

Rebecca is a collector, but also a maker. One of her favourite activities is making fancy things from humble things …

SIMONE BENDIX AND HELENE SCHJERBECK

Paper Castles

With the contented focus of birds making a nest, Danish twins Simone Bendix and Helene Schjerbeck create paper cuttings at the dining table. Chatting constantly, they snip at pages of old books with tiny scissors, creating scenes and objects to decorate the house. Paper offcuts drop around them in a circle like a confetti-lined moat, and every now and again the momentum halts as they throw their heads back in laughter at a shared joke or story. The fifty-year-old twins are paper artists, street performers, poetry ambassadors and the co-owners of a small artisan leathergoods business, Edition Poshette, that aims to spread happiness in the world via a collection of handcrafted bags and accessories.

There are several things that are immediately noticeable about Simone and Helene. Firstly, they often wear identical handmade clothes. Secondly, they laugh a lot and find enormous joy in life. They love to design and make matching outfits, then ride their bikes or stride arm-in-arm across the park. People stop and smile, their delight is mirrored back at them, and the game continues. Whether at a gala in sweeping beige capes and paper crowns, on matching motorbikes with butterfly-laden curly wigs, at a pret-a-porter show wearing books as hats, or at the Palais-Royal in golden dresses and paper necklaces, they are never seen in the same outfits twice. 'This whole idea of sharing and spreading joy has always been very important for us. If we smile and laugh together, if we are present in that tiny moment and enjoy the beauty, we are changing ways of being,' Helene explains.

The only impediment to the fun is the distance between the twins' homes, which they traverse on a regular basis. 'We try to be together as much as possible because we love being together,' says Simone. Helene lives in Tuscany with her Danish husband, Iakob, and their children, Elias and Oscar. Simone lives in Paris with her husband Kasper, who is a musician and composer, and three children, Pablo, Polly and Julian. The sisters move between the two homes regularly, and sometimes meet in Spain where they produce some of their artisan leather range.

Like migratory birds, travel is a natural part of their seasonal rhythms. This is a legacy of growing up in a family that moved and travelled often. From the ages of five to nine, they were based in Rome and attended an international school with a strong focus on books and poetry. On returning to Denmark, they struggled with their native tongue and for a time they were known as 'the spaghetti children'. 'The other children didn't really know how to deal with us because we were just very different, we'd been in a different environment and it took us time to understand each other. For example, we didn't know who Abba was! Instead we had our little stickers of Roman antiquities and pictures of all the monuments,' explains Helene.

Their love of poetry was ignited in Rome and they use this in decorative ways in their homes and creative work. In Simone's Paris apartment, she has created wallpaper from old poetry books to line the walls of the powder room. She frames her favourite poems and hangs them around the house, uses poetry to line leather boxes and suitcases bought from flea markets, and makes poetry papercuts that can be found strung around a lamp shade or down the corridor. In many of the items made for Edition Poshette, they attach a little piece of poetry to the leather, or a few simple words of encouragement such as 'Never Postpone Joy'.

Like many Danish children, the twins grew up with the Hans Christian Andersen fairy tales such as *Thumbelina, The Emperor's New Suit* and *The Little Match Girl*, and also with images of his beautiful paper-cut scenes. Andersen created intricate paper vistas with goblins, skulls, ballerinas and angels. Women on tightropes were also frequent subjects as were oriental castles and mosques with minarets.

Paper-cutting was an important tradition in Helene and Simone's family. They love that is it a pastime that is accessible and egalitarian, something almost everyone can do. 'Nobody is there to say, "Oh, you did it wrong", because the imperfections are really important and actually quite beautiful,' says Helene. They are also passionate about sharing the tradition with others, and marvel at the benefits that making things in the company of others can have. 'When your hands are busy, and when you are focused on something, the things you chat about are completely different to what you would be talking about otherwise,' explains Simone.

Even the process of making a mess, which is a seemingly inconsequential by-product of creating, has its own special meaning. 'Home is a space where I can make a mess, a place where I can make things. So that's the constant. It's transportable to different places and it's still your home,' says Simone. They talk passionately about upcycling – not recycling, but transforming something old into something new. Old maps become wallpaper, vintage books are cut up and transformed into Elizabethan-style collars, headpieces and cuffs, and old scarves become colourful new dresses.

Their mother was a creative homemaker who transported her skills from place to place when they moved. She made her own yoghurt and jam, and approached everything she did with just the right amount of theatre. When she made a loaf of bread, she decorated the top with leaves made from dough, and she taught her children that you don't need a lot of money to add a touch of poetry and beauty to your world. 'Our mother had this saying: "You can always put a rose in your hair",' says Helene.

Simone's home in Paris is infused with a similar spirit. Simone and Kasper bought the apartment in Rue des Martyrs in 2003, when the neighbourhood was full of food shops. 'We loved the "mess" of the area and the buzz of it.' Since then it has become more gentrified but 'it still has a local feel to it, and some really great food shops, so it's easy to get inspired to cook and eat'. Simone and Kasper have decorated the apartment with a mixture of family and flea-market objects, and a jumble of homemade decorations. For Simone, 'objects are just objects until they speak to you, and you answer them by paying respect to the story they are telling you. That's when a home becomes a home and not just a showpiece.' Perhaps she inherited the confidence to create a unique home from her grandmothers, who both shared a deep appreciation for their surroundings. 'One of our grandmothers felt that a day without moving things around was almost wasted.'

Making things for like-minded people, or taking their artwork to the streets to brighten the day of strangers, provides the twins with a way of 'sprinkling poetry into the everyday'. In the same way, home provides them with an opportunity to live inside a poetic world, where the simplest of pleasures and activities provides enough meaning to fill many lifetimes. ◆

'This whole idea of sharing and spreading joy has always been very important for us.'

GREG IRVINE

South Melbourne Sanctuary

Artist Greg Irvine has a fundamental need to live in an environment he finds beautiful. 'I have to be in a world that enchants me. If I lost my eyesight that would be the end of me. I would just have no reason to live.' His 19th-century home is located in the Australian suburb of South Melbourne, and is a vibrant showcase of his artwork and his many varied collections. The single-level house has a small external courtyard framed by palms and cacti, which leads to his painting studio.

'The house is an extension of one of my paintings. Instead of painting with paint, I paint with objects. To me, this whole house is a succession of still lifes, which I change constantly.' Greg arranges each space instinctively and without hesitation. No shelf, drawer or corner escapes his examination. He positions a high-backed Art Nouveau chair by a wall, then throws a silk scarf across one of its wooden arms, its long gold tassels dangling towards the floor, and then plops a vintage velvet cushion on top. It has taken him just a minute, but the assemblage requires no adjustments – it's ready for a close-up.

Greg grew up an only child in a home where art and design were the focus. His mother was a ceramicist by trade, and also an accomplished draftswoman and painter. His father was a milliner who inherited his parents' hat business, which was established in the 1920s in the Australian bayside suburb of Elwood. Together, his parents designed bonnets, boaters, trilbies and sunhats, all handmade on wooden hat blocks and embellished with fine lace and exquisite ribbons. Although none of their hats have survived, Greg's childhood memories of the exquisite fabrics and trims in his parents' factory remain vivid. Unsurprisingly, he later began his own hat collection. It includes

Venetian gondolier hats trimmed with black ribbon, which he uses as wall décor, and a stack of twenty-seven straw hats in a myriad of shades and shapes that occupy a cane chair in his bedroom.

The family home was a place of creativity, but was also marred by emotional difficulties. Greg's father became an alcoholic after serving with the Australian army in World War II and taking part in the brutal conflict with the Japanese in the jungles of Borneo. He returned from the war a different man. He never recovered from the deep trauma of witnessing countless horrors, including the execution of his best friend after an ambush by enemy soldiers. By early 1946, the Australian soldiers had been repatriated home and Greg was born the following year into a home and a nation tarnished by the haunting and dark brush of war.

Whether as a reaction against the difficult atmosphere of the times, or simply due to his own innate optimism and *joie de vivre*, Greg grew up with a strong desire to create lively, colour-filled paintings and a joyous atmosphere in his own home.

Greg's parents did whatever they could to encourage his early creative development. Although his father's addiction gradually consumed him, he continued to nurture his son's interests. He built a cubby house into which Greg installed a small-scale kitchen complete with every possible accoutrement. As a young boy, Greg also spent countless hours beside his mother, playing with clay as she made ceramics for clients. By his early teens, he was deftly shaping the wet clay on the pottery wheel, painting and glazing the results, then operating the kiln in the garage. Clients would visit the home to buy handmade dinner sets, jugs, vases, lamp bases, platters, serving bowls and decorative vessels made by Greg and his mother. Greg was soon making ceramic sculptures, and when he was thirteen one of his pieces won the main prize at the Sun Youth Art Show in Melbourne.

Several years later, his mother saw a newspaper advertisement for the highly respected South Yarra Gallery, which was run by the influential gallerist and art patron, Violet Dulieu, from her expansive 19th-century mansion. With an unwavering belief in her sixteen-year-old son's talents, Greg's mother told him they were 'going to go there and show her your work'. Two years later, Dulieu hosted his first solo exhibition and the show sold out. Greg used the money from his sales to purchase a rare Victorian handcrafted metal birdcage from antique dealer Graham Geddes. He only had $500, but he implored Geddes to sell it to him despite the $800 price tag. Perhaps sympathetic to the teenage boy's passion for unique decorative pieces, Geddes agreed. More than fifty years later, the birdcage still sits proudly in Greg's sitting room.

Greg's early confidence in his art and ceramic work came despite major and potentially debilitating challenges. Throughout his primary and secondary education, his undiagnosed dyslexia was interpreted by his teachers as defiance. He remembers regular beatings, being humiliated in front of other students, and having his drawings torn up in class. 'We don't need artists in here, Irvine!' he was told. While these experiences were difficult, and he felt ostracised by teachers and students alike, his isolation stoked his determination. He knew that his dyslexia would make it difficult to get a regular job. 'It was either be successful as an artist, or die! I had no choice but to be successful, it made me try twice as hard.' He channelled his innate creative abilities, strong work ethic and energy into building a career as an artist. His expertise grew to encompass painting, drawing, mosaics, furniture decoration, and set and costume design.

Greg admits that, while he has created a rich and satisfying life for himself, he has always lived in fear of developing a destructive addiction. Fortunately, the only addiction he has formed is what he laughingly calls his 'very expensive habit of collecting'. His collections range from vintage metal teapots, rare 1920s celluloid thermoplastics, French enamel jugs, tortoiseshell combs and cigarette cases. He also collects Australian enamelware pots, bakelite flatware, bronze Art Nouveau statues and embroidered silk parasols

with hand-carved handles. He collects widely, but is discerning. 'I don't buy randomly. I buy things that go with other things, that I can make a story with.'

History and provenance are important to him. When he was restoring his 19th-century home, he meticulously preserved all its original historic features. He salvaged the wood panels that lined the walls, disintegrating wallpaper, linoleum floors, pressed-tin ceiling panels, the claw-foot bath and even the showerhead. Among the historic objects that liven up each room are valuable antiques and decorative artefacts that span two centuries of design, which he has collected from all over the world. The emerald-green, 19th-century Venetian glass chandelier that sparkles above the dining room table was purchased on one of his many trips abroad. Scottish Art Nouveau armchairs flank the fireplace and beautifully maintained antique cane furniture punctuate many of his rooms.

... Greg's childhood memories of the exquisite fabrics and trims in his parents' factory remain vivid.

While he often collects objects and furniture that are in mint condition, he is also attracted to imperfection. He loves giving broken things a new life in another form. In the early 1990s, nearby Albert Park Lake was dredged and collectors fossicked for glass and porcelain treasures from the Victorian era. Most were searching for unchipped bottles, tiles, glassware and plates, and tossed flawed items to the side. For Greg, the broken fragments were like unfinished sentences that engaged his imagination. Early mornings became archaeological expeditions. He rescued pieces of porcelain and ceramic and brought them home on his bicycle in big sacks. These tiny fragments of domestic history were used to decorate furniture and mirrors, and he created a massive mosaic that covers his courtyard garden.

Greg approaches the maintenance of his home and the creation of his artwork with dedication and commitment. But he also has a strong sense of freedom and amusement, and a desire to evolve and change. His home and studio are both creative sanctuaries and shrines to the very serious business of having fun. ◆

SARAH DE TELIGA

An Apartment on Parc Montsouris

Seven majestic oak trees dominated the front yard of Sarah de Teliga's family home in Australia, and every one of them had a cubby. 'We would hoist up baskets with lunches and dinners using a pulley system. And from the highest platforms we would sprinkle homemade confetti made from flowers and paper circles made with a hole-punch. So I have always lived in trees, in cubby houses, looking down through the branches.'

Decades later, she still has a treetop view of the world from her third-floor Parisian apartment that overlooks the vast Parc Montsouris in the 14th arrondissement. For Sarah, it is a 'bit like a little nest'. She shares the home with her husband, Robert Grace, and it is also where she does much of her painting. From this elevated vantage point, she lives among the park's linden blossom, lime and plane trees. She often paints by the main window in the sitting room, looking onto the park, or *en plein air* among its trees below. She follows the seasonal outpourings of nature closely. 'The colours incremental, morphing into gold. The collapse into suicidal leaf scattering. Then the redemptive hope and renaissance of Frühling/printemps/spring.'

Painting in the park has its challenges, including manoeuvring equipment through snow in the dead of winter, deflecting the unwanted advances of strangers as she works at her easel, and dealing with her own inner voices that can undermine her confidence. 'I'm always in a state of destruction of myself. I can be in the park painting and having a fight with myself – "Well, that's not working, that's not working out!" – and then come back two days later and think, "Yeah it's really working". [As an artist] you're always in confrontation with your limits and your humanity and your ordinariness.'

Sarah's paintings are not simply self-portraits disguised as rocks, trees, planets or ordinary objects. 'I'm always trying to look outside of myself so that I'm not reproducing myself in everything I paint. If I look out the window at a tree, and I keep looking beyond the sense of it, beyond the *presumption* of what it is, and just keep looking at the colour and exactly what's there, I get more of it. I try and remove the preconceptions of what a tree *should* be, so ideally the hand is pushing the mind to evolve.'

Sarah's artistic embrace of Parc Montsouris as one of her most frequent subjects is an uplifting chapter in its dark history. The park was created by Napoleon III in 1867 on a site that included a large stone quarry and a section of the catacombs of Paris. Eight hundred human skeletons were reportedly moved from a network of underground tunnels before work began. Three years later, approximately fifteen acres of land had been transformed into a scenic landscape of undulating hills, rare and native trees, statues, pergolas and a vast lake.

The proximity of the apartment to the park ensures Sarah has continual access to nature, which feeds her work. 'I am an animist, and pray to the shrine of the natural world. All communities need somebody to build a house, somebody to cook and somebody to observe. I've been given the task to observe and show people the little details when they haven't got the time or the opportunity to observe. So that's my job – the observer and the vector.' Some of her paintings combine incongruous subjects such as magnificent trees with dreary-looking rubbish bins, posing questions about human impact on the environment. Works such as *Heart and Dark* (2016) are created in an attempt to illuminate the spirit using symbols of the natural world.

Sarah was born in Tasmania, Australia. She spent her childhood in Melbourne and Sydney, and much of her adult life in France. While technically her home is in Paris, her interior landscape is connected in nature everywhere. 'Home is somewhere I put my mind, where I can paint until the temporal details fade and delicate poetry emerges and where I can focus, meditate and worship. It can be the rockpools in Sydney, megaliths in Cumbria, England, or along the Mediterranean coast of France. All of those outdoor spaces – the sea, the mountains, the forests – connect with my early life as a child in Australia.'

Defining connection to place is one of the main foundations of her work. Part of her yearning for the sometimes harsh Australian landscape is answered by her annual visit to the Cévennes in southern France. 'For two months a year, I go into a wild landscape that's quite arid. It's probably the closest thing here to an Australian landscape, with its wild stunted oak trees surrounded by mountains and rocks.' She paints and draws micro and macro studies there, which can make a tiny clump of lichen appear like a vast landscape, or a pebble appear like a dramatic cliff face. She approaches each rock and tree as though she is painting a portrait. Her interest in studying their forms and colours began in childhood. 'My father was a scientist, a chemist and also a geologist. He'd bring home boxes of chemicals for our laboratory – all different colours, lovely cadmium yellow! "Ooooo, that orange! What is it?" We'd make giant copper-sulphite crystal gardens – as big as we could.'

The chemistry experiments may have also influenced her interest in the changeable qualities of paint and materials. 'I sometimes use phosphorescence in the paint, so that with different light the painting becomes a different thing. I can put a starscape in that doesn't appear until it's dark, so at night it's shining and it's a different painting to the one you see during the day. I once had a client ring me up to say "There's a different painting when I turn the lights off". I'd forgotten to tell her.'

Sarah's unique outlook and free spirit were encouraged by her family. 'We were all pretty wild, there were six of us [siblings] so we did whatever we liked really. It was a free-for-all!' Her grandmother Kath, dubbed 'Circus Granny',

'[As an artist] you're always in confrontation with your limits and your humanity and your ordinariness.'

set the tone with annual visits to Asia, an interest in theosophy and Eastern philosophy, daily yoga including headstands well into her 80s, and the decoration of her home in vivid colours and vibrant silks. 'She was a great colourist and would say things like "I want this really bright yellow. No, no, no, not lemon yellow! The colour of a marigold."' Sarah's mother, Rae, inherited Kath's obsession for colour and installed grass-green carpet throughout the family home, and a sofa upholstered in Marimekko fabric featuring bold purple and turquoise stripes. Sarah remembers finding her mother in tears because she desperately wanted to paint the sitting room a watermelon pink colour and found waiting unbearable. It was painted the following day and peace was restored.

Sarah's uncle, Stan de Teliga, was a landscape painter who worked with an astonishingly beautiful colour palette of muted tertiary hues. He was an active member of the Australian art community and his paintings are held in major collections including the Art Gallery of New South Wales. He was also a staunch defender of Sarah when she was a young art student at East Sydney Technical College (now known as the National Art School) and 'was constantly trying to stop them kicking me out'. Her misdemeanours included 'transforming spaces without permission, flooding the studio with blue paint, and laughing too much'.

Another uncle, John Ogburn, taught painting and drawing at a studio he opened in Sydney in 1963. A decade later he established the influential Harrington Street Artists' Cooperative Gallery. He also worked as an artist himself and his paintings captured international attention.

Sarah approaches paint and colour with joy and veneration. 'People have got millions of images around them, they are submerged in imagery; however nothing can replace paint – the sensuality, the colour and the resonance of paint. When you are in a room with a painting, each day it is a different thing.'

European seasons feel both heightened in their ever-changing sensory offerings, and endless in their winters. 'A lot of my practice is working with the landscape, so the evolution of what's going on outside is what's also going on in the work. It was a hard winter this year with all the assassinations [in Paris], and it never snowed. It was just cold and hard and grim and dark. Everybody sleeps, everybody hibernates.' Fortunately, the colours of her apartment bring spring inside all year round.

A dominating feature of the combined dining–sitting room is a large Liljevalch sofa designed by Joseph Frank in 1934 for Svensk Tenn. The sofa is covered in a heavy linen fabric Frank originally designed in the 1940s, inspired by Persian carpet patterns. 'Mostly his fabrics are related to the natural world. These are beautifully hand-blocked, beautifully coloured.' Sarah's paintings also add colour to the apartment and are hung in pairs or curated in salon-style collections. Alongside the colour is a curated selection of monochromatic and unadorned forms. A white marble dining table designed in 1957 by Finnish industrial designer and architect Eero Saarinen is the central feature of the kitchen, and a black branch, denuded of leaves, drapes across the living room wall. Black-and-white portraits of Sarah and Robert's sons, Linus and Nestor (their names were chosen from Greek mythology), are positioned on desks and tables and a large grey rug covers the sitting room floor.

Sarah's work marries a strength of line and composition with an underlying feeling of openness and vulnerability. Her unique observations of people and nature vacillate between a whisper and shout, protest and celebration, dread and delight. Like a marigold turning its face to the sun, she moves from window to window around the apartment to paint. 'The light starts on one side in the morning and switches to the other in the afternoon. I follow the light.' ◆

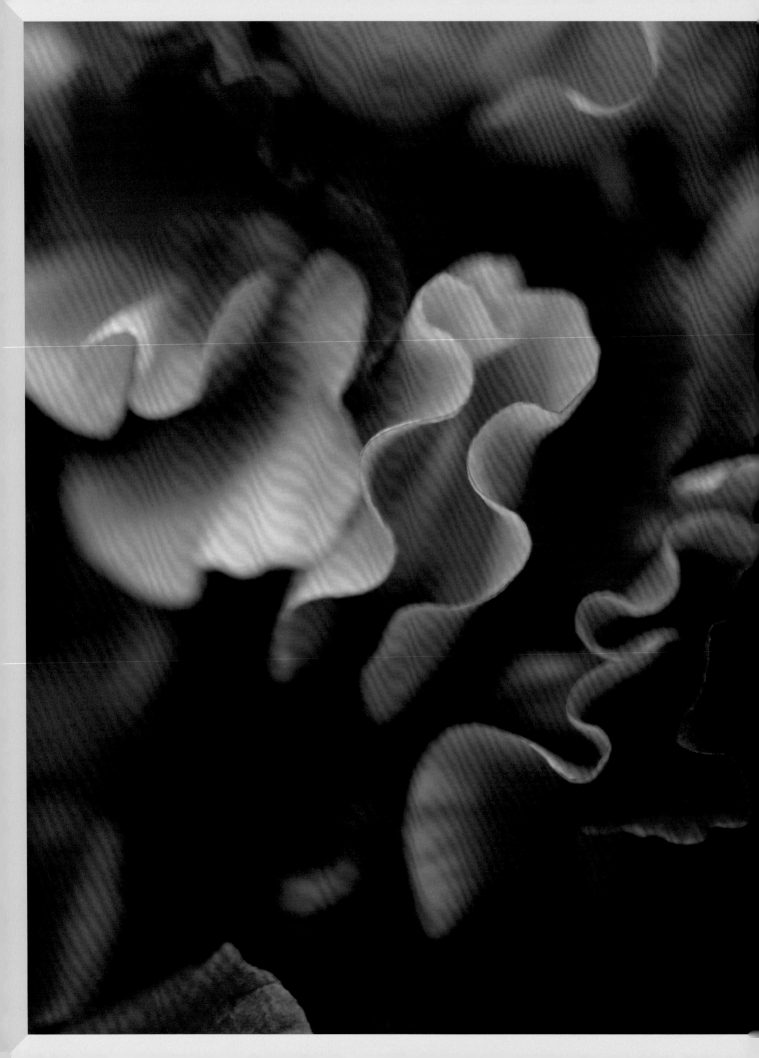

BELLA MEYER

The Art of Flowers, New York

Bella Meyer calls it flower graffiti. It's the gentlest form of guerrilla street art – flowers are randomly given to strangers in New York City. Sometimes small floral bouquets are taped to a pole. Other times they are placed on a wooden bench seat with a tiny handwritten message on cardboard that reads 'Please Take a Flower'. But, more often, single flower stems are handed out with a smile to pedestrians south of Union Square. 'The idea is to go in a group into the streets, into neighbourhoods or spaces such as subway stations, where you wouldn't necessarily see flowers, and go towards people and give them a flower. It creates this utter surprise in them.'

The gesture isn't always welcomed in downtown New York. Wary after years of being accosted on the street, or worried that metaphorical strings might be attached, people sometimes just wave the giver away. 'They either have this moment of joyous surprise, indeed their whole face changes and they happily take the flowers, or they just refuse to accept them.'

For Bella, floral artist and flower graffiti initiator, the impulse to work with flowers began years ago with a wedding announcement. The groom was Jewish and the bride was Catholic/Buddhist. The groom's rabbi didn't want to marry them, so Bella came up with a plan. 'I said, "You should meet this rabbi that I know and I am sure he will marry you." I remember walking out of the meeting, and I was so happy because everyone got along. Out of the blue, I asked, "May I build your chuppah?"'

The couple's floral designer introduced Bella to the New York flower market. 'This was the 1980s, it was extraordinarily rich at that stage. You could find every flower there. The richness of the blooms beaming and shining at you was just unbelievable. I was completely taken by it. I thought, "How can I not respect their miraculous beauty and use them?" So that was the turning point.'

She looked for an avenue to express her passion for flowers. 'I wanted to tell a story with flowers, and very soon I realised I wanted to create something very personal.' She considered having a storefront so she could share her love of flowers with the world. 'The storefront comes from the same idea as flower graffiti. I wanted to give flowers, which is really not lucrative, because I would just like to give flowers away all the time!' Bella found a studio at 55 East 11th Street and completely redesigned the space before opening her floral boutique, Fleurs Bella, in 2010.

At the same time, Bella and her sister were planning the restoration of their family home in France, which they inherited from their mother, Ida. It is located on the Île de la Cité, an island in the Seine, right in the heart of Paris. Bella shipped several pieces of family furniture from the home, and created Fleurs Bella around them. 'I am very attached to the French country furniture inherent to our mother's aesthetic sense. I lived with it growing up and continue to want to be with it.'

The first piece was installed with the help of a friend. 'A huge bookshelf that my mother had – it was tremendous!' It seemed custom-made for the space. 'It happened to fit exactly between two pillars.' Towards the back of the shop are other family heirlooms, including an old French bathtub that is often full of flowers, and an ancient hand basin carved out of stone with a splashback of blue and white tiles.

Each piece of furniture in Bella's studio adds to the personality of the space. A recently installed upright piano – a gift from a friend – prompted her to place a sign outside: 'Please come in and play the piano.' A six-metre-long table, built by a friend from reclaimed timber, runs like a main artery through the heart of the space. Flower designers move along either side in a gentle dance, reaching for seasonal blooms from buckets and vases that line the walls to prepare customer orders.

Entering the studio is less like being in a shop and more like walking into a tiny oasis. 'I like to change spaces around and give an element of surprise to people, an element of joy. And how do you give that? You invite people into a world of wonderment, an enchanted world.' An abundant array of flowers decorates the shop in varying seasonal colour palettes. Bella particularly loves garden roses, peonies, field flowers, orchids and ranunculuses, but she also works with heavily textured forms like dry reeds, bark, rocks, cacti, lichen, wavy branches and tree trunks.

Before becoming a floral designer, Bella wore many other hats. She taught medieval art history in Paris and then moved to New York where she worked at the French embassy and was responsible for visual arts. She also created masks and designed theatre costumes. 'I started with puppetry – creating the stories, designing and making the puppets and making their environments.' In some ways, her previous experiences have helped her create a studio that is part theatre and part art installation.

Her earliest memories of flowers are from the south of France. 'I always had a love of flowers. I was enchanted by things growing – just looking at them in wonderment. I remember sitting outside as a child looking at minuscule flowers.' Her interest was deepened in the home of her grandfather, artist Marc Chagall, whom she visited often with her mother. 'Whenever we would go to see him we would *always* bring flowers. We would stop at the village nearby and buy flowers at the market. They were simple – a big bunch of flowers – and he would marvel at them.'

Chagall believed flowers were the epitome of beauty. He often depicted their blooms and foliage in his work, perhaps understanding their colours and textures more fully by painting them. The fleeting and delicate splendour of the bouquets, and the memories they represent, are now preserved forever in his work. *Bouquet près de la fenêtre* (*Flowers by the Window*, 1959–60) is dominated by an unstructured arrangement of flowers in every colour, and *La Baou de Saint-Jeannet* (*The Baou of Saint-Jeannet*, 1969), features a giant bouquet framed against a deep blue night sky with the village of Saint-Jeannet in the background. In *La Baie des Anges* (*The Bay of Angels*, 1962), a mermaid holds a huge bunch of flowers as she floats in the air above the Côte d'Azur.

Her earliest memories of flowers are from the south of France ... Her interest was deepened in the home of her grandfather, artist Marc Chagall ...

As a child, Bella would sometimes imagine herself disappearing into one of her grandfather's paintings. 'The places I cherish the most are very intimate places found in my grandfather's paintings. They were like my fairytale world. I loved sitting next to him watching him paint, wondering what would next appear on the canvas.'

Bella's mother had also spent her childhood immersed in Chagall's work, and Ida developed a strong affinity for painting. In a 1949 photograph, one of Ida's paintings can be seen leaning against a wall alongside two paintings by her father. 'She grew up in the studio, so she painted. She was a wonderful, wonderful painter and had several exhibitions. But it was hard to do it because she had to do things for her father, especially after her mother died. She was very much involved with helping him with his work, from the stage designs he was doing, or trying to get in touch with dealers or museum curators. Eventually she stopped painting completely. When he needed her, she was there.'

As Bella got older, she continued to visit her grandfather regularly. He shared his advice and wisdom, but shielded her from his most difficult and painful memories, never speaking for example of the sadness he felt when her grandmother died. Chagall believed in being guided by the heart not the head, and he encouraged his grandchildren to take a similar approach in their own lives. 'I would visit him frequently. I needed to hear him talk about the simple things in life, about the *ideal* of the simple things. I was very insecure and hesitant and shy and I needed his encouragement, and his fervent belief in listening to one's heart.'

Bella has managed to create the feeling of village life in her corner of New York City. Her studio is just a five-minute walk from her apartment, which is another peaceful haven, despite being close to the constant hum of Union Square and the chaos of Broadway. At home, the room that resonates most with Bella is the combined sitting room, library and office. The décor includes mid-century furniture and antiques, and piles of books, papers and folders sit on tables and on the floor. Handmade masks mingle with art books, woven baskets, wooden artefacts and ceramics on two large white shelves. Chagall's paintings hang on the wall, and his photograph appears with other family memorabilia around the room. Gentle light comes in through giant windows and a jungle of indoor plants and flowers grow in pots. Bella often works or paints in this room, at a large desk that once belonged to Chagall. One of her mother's paintings is positioned at eye level near the desk, as if overseeing the activities that take place there.

Perhaps on some level, the spirit of this room reminds Bella of the world her grandfather inhabited: a simple world, where light, painting, flowers and family intersected to create a daily rhythm. When Chagall died in 1985, at the age of ninety-seven, Bella was thirty years old. Her memories of him remain vivid. 'His desk, which is actually now my desk, was in front of the window, which had beautiful light coming in from the Côte d'Azur. He had several easels – big, big easels. And there was a large table in the middle, and tons of papers, and the different things he would draw. He would sit at his desk or in front of one of his easels, and he would work and paint, and there were always flowers.'

In Chagall's painting *Bella à l'oeillet* (*Bella with a Carnation*, 1925), Chagall's wife and muse looks out to the world with thoughtful, intelligent eyes. Her pale face is framed by brunette hair cropped in a short bob. She holds a single flower stem in her left hand. The bloom is iridescent white against her dark dress. It could almost be mistaken for a portrait of her namesake and granddaughter, Bella Meyer, almost a century later, as she prepares to hand a flower, and a little moment of joy, to a stranger on the streets of New York. ◆

GIOVANNA CARBONI

An Apartment in Milan

A snake sits on the shelf in a bottle of formaldehyde. It's a small python with golden skin and a wavy pattern that runs the length of its body. If it wasn't in a wine bottle sealed with a messy lattice of red wax drippings and decorated with a cream ribbon bow, it could be mistaken for a museum specimen.

Giovanna Carboni lives outside the norms of northern Italian society. Her interests are different from those of most women in Milan, which is one of Italy's most traditional and conservative cities. 'I have a weird love for *wunderkammer*-like objects, which is why the entire house could be confused as a cabinet of curiosities. There are taxidermy animals, biological specimens in glass and mysterious powders retrieved from chemistry labs that have closed. Anatomy, science and astronomy are not my expertise, but I have a genuine passion for them.' Her home is also decorated with 19th-century scientific illustrations of the human body, mixed in with historic and contemporary art works, found objects, and Giovanna's own furniture designs.

Giovanna lives with her partner, musician and restaurateur Sergio Carnevale, and their baby son, Giotto. Their apartment is located on Milan's Naviglio Grande in the neighbourhood known as the Quartiere Navigli. The area is a thriving enclave of artists, photographers, musicians and industrial and fashion designers. A warren of tiny cobblestoned streets leads to hundreds of internal courtyards that hide many of the most interesting creative spaces in Milan.

The industrious creative scene is matched by a boisterous nightlife, much of which is set around the waterways. Historically, the canals were established for practical reasons. In 1482, Leonardo da Vinci was commissioned to design a canal system to connect Milan with the natural rivers and water sources of wider Lombardy.

The new canals enabled shipments of prized, light pink and white Candoglian marble from Lake Maggiore to be transported into the city centre to build the city's famous Gothic cathedral, the Duomo di Milano. Many of the original canals have now been covered by roads, but Giovanna has a view from her apartment of the largest of the three remaining main canals, which leads to the one of the city's historic gates, Porta Ticinese.

As the daughter of passionate antique collectors, Giovanna embraces the history of the area. She followed in her father's footsteps and studied architecture, but she now spends much of her time restoring and recreating furniture, giving neglected pieces new life. 'My job is unearthing antiques and, when possible, reinventing them. I create unique pieces, new functional hybrids of antiquities using contemporary materials and techniques. My aim is to breathe new life into old objects, while reshaping their functionality and purposes.'

Giovanna remembers a childhood filled not with playgrounds and church on Sundays, but 'wandering for antiques and going to brocantage markets all around Italy and Europe with my family'. The décor in her bedroom was very different to that of her friends. 'It would not have met many people's expectations of a child's bedroom! It had a serious tone: my parents had furnished it with big, antique pieces of furniture and décor, which some children may have found intimidating. The floor was always covered with toys, so my sister and I grew up in that environment, and were happy amongst those things.' For Giovanna, being surrounded by antique furniture not only represented the past but was 'somehow reassuring of a long future in front of me'.

Each piece of furniture that she works on has its own special character and personality, from her dining room table to the armoire she created by combining a 17th-century shelf with antique doors from the same era. 'I have an innate, almost mad attitude towards anthropomorphising furniture. Most of the old design pieces have their silent, personal story to tell, and they communicate it to me through their solidity, beauty and resilience to children's attacks. I want to continue the story and refurbish not only their shape, but also their function.'

Today, Milan's design culture is globally renowned, encouraged substantially by the annual design fair, Salone del Mobile, but Giovanna's furniture designs are not part of this movement. She is not motivated by designing the next streamlined chair or award-winning seasonal must-have. Instead, she rescues historic pieces from demise. 'Nowadays, people tend to prefer new designer furniture to antiques, and are forgetting the historical, artistic and social value of craftsmanship. Italy retained a unique ability in merging art with design, and is still full of old beauty which now seems doomed to be forgotten. I want people, particularly the young, to rediscover it. Recycling, reinventing antiques. It's a mission!'

Giovanna's apartment provided her with another avenue to put her principles into practice. 'Would you believe the previous owners preferred the 1980s linoleum floor to the original, antique parquetry and stone floorings you see now under our feet? Can you imagine my surprise when I got rid of that horrible floor covering?'

The apartment is in a constant state of change, with furniture coming and going depending what she is working on. 'It's my living portfolio and studio, where clients can come and even buy pieces of furniture shown and see how it is used in a real-life context. Its metamorphosis is due to a dynamic turnover of objects that I buy, recreate and sell to private clients who have a particular style, and an appreciation for sober beauty.'

While Giovanna takes her rescue-and-restore mission very seriously, clues to the exuberant and uninhibited side of her personality are also dotted around her apartment. Her substantial hat collection, in a rainbow of colours and shapes, is found in little groupings around the apartment, and messages of love for her husband have been scratched into the wall of their shared office. Naked porcelain dolls sit wide-legged on top of vintage books, and a set of plaster teeth sits on the mantelpiece, clenching a rose.

Sergio's interests add even more personality to their home. One of the dominant features of the main dining and living area is the grand piano and a large, round drum sits on the floor nearby – unsurprisingly, music fills their home. Giovanna and Sergio seem able to embrace everything Milan has to offer, without being impeded by the centuries-old codes of behaviour and tradition that weigh heavily on the shoulders of many other residents. They live to their own rhythm and have created a unique and wonderful world by combining creativity and music, history and the present.

'We live in a smart city, capable of absorbing and retaining culture from its past, but also of evolving and progressing in new directions. Milan might be a bit too fixed on certain standards of behaving and living, and can even exhibit a vain, showy style. I am lucky enough to feel free of all that. I have never felt I had to satisfy any expectations from other people, critics, alleged experts or the handyman.' ◆

LUKE SCIBERRAS

The House at Hill End

'The sense of home, to me, is very, very precious,' says artist Luke Sciberras. 'It's paramount to the feeling of having a springboard, like having an embracing family that supports you. Whichever direction my work in the studio takes me, I can use the colour and content of this place to feel the energy that it needs.'

On first impressions, Luke's home and studio exude an eclectic and multi-layered ramshackle feel, but it becomes apparent over time that he carefully curates everything into a series of still lifes. A tableau of garden flowers in various stages of decay sits on the dining table, and dozens of artworks and handcrafted objects fill the room like clues to private memories and intimate encounters. 'Everything around me has to have a reason to be here. I can tell you a story about every object.'

His home is located in the small town of Hill End, about four hours north-west of Sydney, over the Blue Mountains. Gallerist Scott Livesey believes that Luke has become the custodian of the town's ongoing affair with Australian art. 'I don't know another painter who is so respectful of the lineage of Australian painters and certainly not just those at Hill End. His knowledge of the language of paint and painters is quite extraordinary.'

Hill End was once a booming gold mining town of 10,000 people, thanks in part to the 1872 discovery of a 3000-ounce gold nugget. Today, it has a population of fewer than 200 people. There are few cars on the road, and the town's original architecture and wind-worn fences give it the feel of an historic town petrified in a time capsule.

Luke first visited Hill End as an art student in 1997. He went with a group of classmates and lecturers from Sydney Technical College (now known as the National Art School). Having seen the 1995

Artists of Hill End exhibition at the Art Gallery of NSW, he was intrigued. 'The [Russell] Drysdales had a richness and a desolation and a romance, all at the same time. That really appealed to me.' He set off on the excursion inland with a mixture of curiosity and scepticism. It was a rite of passage for the young artists. They were following in the footsteps of several generations of Australian artists before them, including John Olsen, Brett Whiteley, Jeffrey Smart and Margaret Olley. Luke was captivated. 'One of the most appealing things about the place was that the locals have always seen people for exactly who they are. They take it or leave it, but they are not terribly judgemental.' At that time, he was a skinny art student with mad clothes and long hair. 'I was pretty crazy, but I got the feeling immediately that the locals just said "Right, well, that's the guy who does that. He's like that. That's who he is."'

Luke settled permanently in Hill End in 2000 with his former wife, artist Gria Shead, and their daughter, Stella. He remembers the moment he saw their house for the first time. 'I stood at the gate and looked up the front path of the house and there was a full rainbow arching right over it! I knew that minute that it was mine.' The 1873 Georgian cottage was constructed with a combination of saplings and mud using an ancient composite technique known as wattle and daub. 'It was a nicely proportioned cottage that had a checkered history and I felt happy to add a new chapter.' The building was surrounded by an overgrowth of swaying grasses and had been unoccupied for a long time. The only signs of its former life were a large apricot tree in the front yard and a thriving lemon tree out the back.

Luke and Gria bought the house and later leased a nearby stone church to use as a shared studio. 'It was very run down, completely derelict, but we thought it would be good because it's close to the house.' The bishop 'came with his robes and crosses' to deconsecrate and thank the building before handing over its care to the artists. Resident swallows and rabbits moved to new quarters, along with the church pews, bibles and doilies. Crumbling windows were replaced and walls were replastered. In 2009, Luke bought the building.

The expansive space makes an ideal studio for multiple easels, allowing him to move easily between a number of works in progress. Luke has populated the space with his collections of bones, books, sculptures, skulls and stones. 'In the studio, there are objects that I have a very strong attachment to, not in any materialistic sense, but they are sentimental. And looking at an object from somewhere I have been is as evocative as looking at a drawing or a photograph. There's a story in everything and what I do is tell stories.'

The interiors of both his home and studio are crucial to his state of mind. 'I can't relax in a sterile environment or a careless environment. It makes me depressed. It makes me sad. It doesn't have to be lavish or pretentious, but if there's care then you can feel it.' He may have inherited this aspect of his character from his mother, who has always had a deep interest in art and interiors. He remembers his own childhood bedroom fondly, describing it as 'actually rather like a museum. I always collected fossils and geological items of interest as well as birds and fragments of dead animals. My room was kind of weird. My mother has very good taste, but my room was always like *The Addams Family* wing of the house!'

Luke grew up on the edge of bushland and felt very much at home there. 'I'd be on my little BMX bike and be in the bush within about ten minutes. I collected anything with a pattern or texture.' His senses were awakened among the trees and rocks and very little escaped his attentive examination. 'It might have been the weight of a rock, or the shape of a leaf, or the colour of a piece of bark, or the light in a piece of sap. These were tiny beautiful little worlds that I used to like to dive into.'

Years later, similar natural elements and forms attracted him to Hill End, and in the early days he painted the surrounding landscapes incessantly. When he is not working in the landscape, he likes to start a painting by holding an object he found

'Everything around me has to have a reason to be here. I can tell you a story about every object.'

there. 'The way that things are made in nature and the evidence of that has always been intriguing to me – the density of the bones in an animal, and the anatomy and scientific make-up of things.' This abiding curiosity has served him well as an artist. It informs his work, whether he is painting a body of water, a craggy mountain landscape or an animal.

As a teenager, Luke became a fixture in the homes and studios of artists who lived in nearby Wedderburn, south of Sydney. 'There was a group of artists there: John Peart, Elisabeth Cummings, Suzanne Archer and David Fairbairn. They had a wonderful flair and freedom I really responded to. It's funny how you just sort of slip into a tribe of people who you find an immediate affinity with.' Elisabeth gave him private drawing lessons, and they used to go up on the roof of her house to draw. A tender portrait of seventeen-year-old Luke, painted by Elisabeth, now hangs on his dining room wall.

Elisabeth also encouraged Luke to attend art school in Sydney, and he has since found his place in the long tradition of Australian landscape painters. Livesey believes Luke's strong relationships with other artists will ensure that his work continues to develop. 'He knocks around with some fairly serious painters and artists and I'm sure they joust and keep each other in check. This camaraderie has helped expand his art practice.'

Luke's residencies and art adventures have taken him around the world and deep into the Australian landscape. He has worked *en plein air* from the Flinders Ranges in South Australia to the arid terrain of the Tanami desert, which straddles the Northern Territory and Western Australia. He has also painted in Wilcannia, set on the shores of the Darling River, and Bruny Island in Tasmania. He often goes on painting excursions with other artists, sometimes to remote and inaccessible areas like Cape York and Thursday Island, which he visited with artist John Olsen. But he always loves coming home.

Luke's paintings are akin to a gathering and layering of memories that builds up on the canvas over time. 'Those flickering decisions made during the process of creating a painting are all triggered and stimulated by objects that I find in my travels – stones, feathers, shards of notepaper, it doesn't matter what it is. But it means something to me and takes me back to the place that I'm making a painting about, even more than a photograph.'

He talks about the process of painting the way a chef might describe inventing a new dish, using a myriad of sensory and intuitive decisions. 'When you are making a painting, you are making bodily decisions. It might just be the flip of a knife moving across a couple of colours, and it might be the tone, or the temperature of a colour that you can add to a painting in dozens of different ways. It could be a runny glaze, the consistency of red cordial, or thick and creamy like blobs of sour cream. There are so many ingredients and techniques, rather like cooking.'

Unsurprisingly Luke is also a passionate cook. His kitchen and studio feel like two separate chambers of the same heart. His cooking inspires his painting, and the colours, textures and pleasures of painting inspire what he creates in the kitchen. Plucked chickens, freshly caught squid, and animal bones and hooves are the subjects of the paintings that adorn the kitchen walls along with a handsome collection of old pots, pans, iron spoons, forks and knives.

He entertains regularly, sometimes catching, hunting or fishing for the main ingredients. He harvests a selection of fruit and vegetables from his garden, which he grows as much out of necessity as pleasure. Artichokes, apricots, almonds, mulberries, mint, kale and quince are just some of his homegrown produce. This close relationship between food and art saw him make a rare foray into the commercial world in 2012, when he created the illustrations for *The Art of Pasta* with his friend, Sydney restaurateur Lucio Galletto. Pea tendrils swirling, beetroots bleeding and prawns drawn on a white tablecloth accompanied the recipes.

Luke loves the feeling of one dish becoming another, linked by stories and memories as ingredients are used in different ways. 'The history of one dish can stretch back for days and days. For example, if you make a beautiful rooster stock, then take the flesh from the rooster and put it aside, you can use the stock in a risotto and then the next day make a pie with the flesh of the rooster.'

Despite the isolation of Hill End, Luke Sciberras never wants for company. Whether passing time with Gria and Stella when they come from Sydney; spending an afternoon at the pub surrounded by a dozen locals; or cooking for visiting artist friends, the offerings from his garden and kitchen will continue to be as abundant as his social life. Similarly, his artwork will keep feeding those who are hungry for the magic of the Australian landscape. ◆

MARCO AROSIO

A Villa in Milan

Milan was quiet in the pre-dawn darkness. Churchgoers were not yet awake or dressing in their elegant outfits for the Sunday service, and baristas had not started making coffees, but seventeen-year-old Marco Arosio had already left the house. In a bag he carried valuable silverware, crystal and ceramics from his parents' cabinets, determined to sell them for a good price.

Marco's late father was a doctor who often received lavish gifts from grateful patients whose lives he had helped to save. Marco's mother is an artist, like her mother before her, and her emotional state has always been deeply affected by the aesthetics of things around her. She is rapturous about beautiful things and repulsed by objects she feels are unappealing. Many of the gifts her husband received did not pass her stringent aesthetic criteria. Unable to live with objects she found ugly, she would ask Marco to take them to the Mercato del Naviglio Grande, Milan's antique and flea market, and sell them.

Marco needed little encouragement. He knew from a very young age that he wanted to be an antique dealer. He was twelve when he saw a photograph in *Grazia* magazine that changed his life. The image was part of a story about designer Piero Fornasetti, and it featured an arched window Piero had built in a room in his house in Milan. The window was lined with clear glass shelves and filled with a collection of precious multicoloured Bohemian goblets. Marco's obsession with glass was born from this image of light filtering through the coloured vessels and the memory has never left him.

Hungry to learn, the market trips as a teenager provided him with an informal education. He usually came back from the market triumphant, although sometimes he returned with objects of refined design to replace those banished from the house. He soon began to move further afield, to the markets of France and Belgium, and developed a love of Art Nouveau and Art Deco glasses and ceramics. He eventually became an expert in decorative art and European ceramics of the 20th century, Murano glass from the 1890s to the 1970s, Art Nouveau French glass and Tiffany and Austrian glass.

The Mercato is an institution in Milan. For regulars, it is also a community. 'I have people who remember me, even thirty years later, and they say, "I remember you, you were at the flea market close to the Naviglio."' The market is still held once a month, set up on either side of one of the city's last remaining canals, near Porto Genova. Storeholders sell everything from furniture to vintage clothes, antiques and jewellery and the theatre of the market continues to be a microcosm of Italian life. 'I remember in the 1980s, the Italian Prime Minister Craxi was at the market, standing at the table next to mine. He bought a Russian icon, framed in silver, at the market as a gift for the Pope – can you imagine? Bought at a flea market!'

Marco now lives in a three-storey villa next to a small canal, the Naviglio della Martesana, in Gorla. Gorla was once a small rural village but it is now part of Milan's north-eastern suburbs. His great-grandfather, Arturo Monti, bought the home in 1934. Arturo suffered from what Marco describes as a congenital family passion for art. He bought the villa to give his only daughter, Maria Monti, an alternative to studying art. 'My grandmother had not been able to attend Brera Academy of Art in Milan, which was at the time considered an unsuitable place for a young woman from a good family.' Arturo's dream was to live with his four children and his wife, Maria Teresa, in a place where their daughter could paint.

Arturo purchased the villa and its extensive 1500-square-metre garden from Karl Singer, an Austrian who built it both as a family home and a workshop where he distilled fine perfumes, essences and specialist liqueurs. 'Some people still remember the boats floating on the Martesana with crates of dried essences and roots, ready to be treated and used to create precious fragrances.' The boatmen would unload the materials directly into the house through a large window that opened onto the canal.

For ten years, life in the villa was everything Arturo had hoped it would be, centred on art and its inspiration. It became the gathering place for his friends, such as Italian artists Giuseppe Palanti and Guido Tallone. His daughter painted *en plein air*, as he had dreamed she would, and Maria Teresa created an inspiring, scented garden including lilla, osmanthus and calicantus. Central to Maria's planting scheme was the idea that something should always be in flower. Early photographs show pines, cedars and other coniferous trees, fruit trees, and more exotic varieties such as bamboo and yucca plants. An enormous original lime tree, European fan palm, and a large, shady magnolia still play centre stage in the middle of the back lawn.

This peaceful, idyllic life came to a devastating halt on 20 October 1944, when a bomb destroyed the primary school next door. The school took a direct hit; the bomb killed 184 schoolchildren and trapped many of them under tons of rubble. Nineteen adults were killed, including teachers, staff, and mothers who had run to the school with their younger children when the air-raid alarms sounded. Constant reminders of the horrors of the bombing and its aftermath, and memories of the children who became known as 'the little martyrs of Gorla', were painful for the family to live with. For many years, their experience of the villa was tarnished with the sadness of that event.

In 1992, when Marco was twenty-seven, he was offered the opportunity to move into the villa. Nearly half a century had passed since the war, and it felt like the right time to breathe new life and optimism into the neglected home and garden.

By then, Marco was well-versed in the world of 20th-century furniture, glass and ceramics from Italy, France, Austria and England, giving him the credentials to faithfully restore the property. Like his mother, Marco felt strongly about surrounding himself with beautiful objects and interiors. He began by correcting the 'vulgar restorations' overseen by various caretakers between the end of the war and his arrival. He replaced or repaired the interiors and commenced work on the garden, which had been almost completely destroyed.

One of the biggest changes he made was the installation of 300 square metres of 1920s floor tiles that he bought from a hotel near Lake Maggiore, north of Milan, that was closing down. 'For me, the tiles, or the flooring, is the most important thing for an interior. The original ones in the house were far more simple, and in very bad condition.' He added favourite furniture pieces, artisanal light fixtures and family heirlooms and hand-me-downs. 'I have many pieces of furniture that are not incredible quality, but they come from my family, so I say, "Okay, come back home boys to the place where you were born!"'

Colour is one of Marco's great obsessions and, like his mother and grandmother before him, he has a strong instinct for using it to create mood. 'I noticed that because the house was so full of light I had the opportunity to use very unexpected colours.' Inspired by colours he saw inside the Copenhagen home of the late Danish sculptor Bertel Thorvaldsen, he chose specific hues for each room. 'I was very, very impressed by the series of rooms in three colours at Thorvaldsen's. One was a Pompeii red, another was painted an English green and another is a very strong yellow colour. Seeing this changed something in me.'

Marco commissioned artists Roberto Renzi and Roberto Reale to cover the semicircular entrance hall with wallpaper, using the pages of old books. On the left of the entrance is a deep-turquoise reception room dominated by a 1930s Murano chandelier, which is framed by a mottled

> For ten years, life in the villa was everything Arturo had hoped it would be, centred on art and its inspiration.

stained-glass window. Almost a century ago, this was the window used as a receiving area for goods delivered by water from the canal below for Singer's perfume and liqueur business. A light-filled sunroom is painted in a soft fern-green, furnished with a small, round wrought-iron table and chairs, and decorated with Fornasetti trays and plates that climb up the walls and cover the ceiling. Next to the vast formal dining room is a small, cosy sitting room with green striped wallpaper, followed by another living area with deep ocean-green walls and objects and furniture that are awash in a sea of magenta.

Rare and quirky objects feature throughout the house, including a handcrafted porcelain dinnerware set designed by Gio Ponti in the 1920s, when he was the director of the historic ceramic company Richard Ginori. The individual plates are mounted on the wall in a small lavender-coloured dining room, positioned in a symmetrical fan pattern above antique furniture. The same room also features two ornate French bronze candelabras and an antique clock Marco purchased at auction in 2007. The pieces once decorated the Via Buonarroti apartment where Maria Callas lived in the 1950s. Marco's enduring love for the design of Fornasetti is evident in a number of rooms, with furniture by both Barnaba and Piero Fornasetti and Fornasetti vases, ashtrays and wallpaper at every turn.

Marco curates artworks, salon-style, throughout the house. Paintings by his mother and grandmother, sketchbook drawings in flea-market frames, and images by German photographer Candida Höfer mix with historic paintings, works by local artist friends and the occasional modern masterpiece. Photographic works feature prominently, including some by Massimo Vitali, Luigi Ontani and Vittorio Pescatori. The images are complemented by carefully positioned ceramic works by sculptor Giuseppe Ducrot, Rome-based artist Giosetta Fioroni, and writer and sculptor Fausto Melotti.

The villa's large rear verandah can be accessed from many of the rooms through large wrought-iron framed glass doors. Concrete balustrades support the pergola, which is covered with a wispy tide of wisteria. When preparing the house for one of the many events and parties, Marco can invariably be found here, carefully pruning the deep pink climbing roses or cutting flowers from the garden at a large outdoor table and arranging them in vases around the house.

Marco finds great meaning in his restoration of his great-grandmother's garden design. He commissioned Tommaso Scacchi to build a white lacquered gazebo based on the original drawings, and he also installed rare 19th-century iron chairs, statues and vases. 'Following the vision of my great-grandparents, I have also tried to plant the garden in such a way that there is always something in flower.'
In January, when the garden is still dormant in the foggy greyness of the Milan winter, small yellow Japanese allspice flowers appear like tiny signs of the colour to come. Bulbs and peonies are next, followed by hydrangeas and a chorus of rose varieties that continue to blossom until November.

Stepping inside the villa, it feels as if time has stood still. Just as it was before the war, the house is infused with colour, art and atmosphere, and filled with a constant stream of guests. Arturo would have been pleased to know that his great-grandson loves the villa as much as he did, and that once again it has become a meeting place for artists. In 1944, it was probably impossible to imagine the scars of the bombing would ever heal. Yet, in a quiet triumph over that dark day in the history of Gorla, children are again celebrated at Villa Singer. 'With the help of my family, the home has again become the centre of our affections. In the garden, we have planted new fruit trees for every grandchild that has arrived.' ◆

> Stepping inside the villa, it feels like time has stood still. Just as it was before the war, the house is infused with colour, art and atmosphere

PAIGE STEVENSON

The House of Collection

In 1989, when Paige Stevenson moved into a semi-abandoned industrial building in Williamsburg, New York, the neighbourhood was considered a no-go zone. Taxis refused to service the area for fear of being car-jacked, thieves stripped stolen cars of parts then set their naked shells alight in the street, and on weekends the area was virtually abandoned, littered with evidence of a thriving local crack cocaine trade. Creature comforts in the area were virtually non-existent; fashionable boutiques and cafes were still more than twenty years away.

Paige and her three artist friends moved into the sixth floor, which had been empty and derelict for years. There were broken windows, rubble everywhere, and bees regularly flew in from a hive that an artist kept on the roof. It wasn't long until the 1500-square-metre loft space was a bustling centre of communal living. At its busiest, it housed ten people who shared just one bathroom. Later, after her original housemates had moved on, Paige divided the space into several separate dwellings, retaining almost half of the area to share with a changing array of friends, more than sixty indoor plants, and her two cats. She calls the loft the House of Collection, and virtually every inch of the space is covered in an eclectic assemblage of objects.

Paige, whose interests include Middle Eastern and fire fan dancing, hosting gatherings, and exploring and collecting, has always encouraged like-minded friends and artists to use the space. 'My formative years were spent living communally, and I still have the sense that people are happier when they feel connected to each other and have some level of common purpose.' She grew up in the drag and hippy culture of Northern California in the late 1960s and early 70s, moving from place to place with her parents as they experimented with various ways of living.

She lived for a while in a commune near Point Arena called The Land, where they slept in a tipi. 'My mother had done some babysitting to trade for a traditional native-style tipi and a small camper which the community helped us set up, and it was a really idyllic time for me. I enjoyed the freedom and the sense of community, and I think I have tried to replicate that feeling in the House of Collection. I was young enough to be really impressed, and while that was my experience of the world, I grew to understand that it wasn't the norm. But I always go back to communal living as an ideal.' Later, Paige moved with her father and his new partner, Dina, to a goat farm where they made soft cheeses and raised chickens. The property was nestled into the edge of a redwood forest, looking out on sheep pastures. 'It was magical to spend time alone in those woods as a child. It made an impression on me.'

In the early 1970s they moved again, this time into a house in San Francisco's Haight-Ashbury neighbourhood with friends of Dina. Paige remembers her room was a converted bathroom 'with my bed on top of the bathtub!' They lived with Dina's cousin, Billy Orchid, who was a member of a cult drag performance group called the Cockettes that performed at the Pagoda Palace Theater in North Beach. The Cockettes' charismatic hippy leader, Hibiscus (George Edgerly Harris II), encouraged the anti-consumer concept that audience members should attend their performances for free. Bearded, glittering, bejewelled and sometimes partially clothed drag queens introduced their previously underground culture to the broader American public for the first time. Their wild, subversive, and often drug-fuelled performances became a magnet for the Californian counterculture, and a focus for those wanting freedom and fun. 'As gay flower children, they had a head start at shucking the constrictive norms of post-World War II America, but they maintained a certain innocence.'

After Hibiscus abandoned the group, the Cockettes debuted in New York to an audience that included Andy Warhol, Truman Capote, John Lennon and Yoko Ono. The media was disdainful, although Diana Vreeland admired their flamboyant costumes and outlandish behaviour and was one of many influential Manhattan hostesses who entertained the group during their visit.

Paige remembers the Cockettes embracing the magic of her childhood games and activities as much as she did. 'They dressed up, there were flowers, and glitter beards – everyone was playing dress-ups along with me.' The wonderful cast of characters left a deep impression on her. 'There was one person I remember specifically, her name was Pristine Condition, and she had an amazingly beautiful Victorian apartment with a bust of Napoleon that would be dressed in different over-the-top outfits every time there was a party.'

Paige's childhood prepared her well for the rudimentary facilities in her Williamsburg loft. She had spent much of her early life living literally off the grid. 'On the goat farm, we did not have electricity, and did not have hot water, so I am not afraid of that. I don't feel like I have to have a lot of things that other people are dependent on. I appreciate them, but I know I'd be fine without them, so that's actually an empowering thing because I don't feel trapped by my needs and my dependencies. I know that I can live in many different ways.'

Similarly, her parents' anti-consumerist philosophy helped equip Paige for life in industrial Williamsburg where there was barely a shop in sight. Her parents referred to themselves as downwardly mobile as 'they didn't want to have anything to do with the baby-boomer cultural mandate of consuming, owning and buying'. In the late 1970s, they moved to Portugal for several years, where American consumer culture was not yet the norm. 'People were still using tools they had been using for hundreds of years, washing things in the same way, doing things like they had been doing them forever. It was a departure from

disposable culture. The things that were really valuable were handmade and took time to create. I wonder if that is the reason why I appreciate old things?' Paige's Portuguese friends seemed innocently unaware of the empty promises of consumerist products. 'Everything modern and American was by definition cool to them, and since this made me cool in their eyes I kept my differing opinions to myself.'

Perhaps as a result of these influences, Paige's home feels like an homage to a pre-industrial America. Tools, handmade furniture, salvaged broken treasures and rescued artefacts from other times create a space that she describes as a constantly changing 'living organism'. The treasures that decorate her walls, ceilings and windowsills were found in abandoned buildings in upstate New York, Pennsylvania and Connecticut and as far away as Nova Scotia. 'Things were just left there to decay and somebody needed to save them, and appreciate them, and love them, so I did that for many years. There is a tradition on American farms of displaying tools and animal remains on barn walls, so what I have done is really an extension of that.'

Her first memories of collecting are from her high school years, when she playfully embraced the role of entropy warrior. Later, when she moved to college, she didn't arrive with all the new and shiny accoutrements commonly purchased by anxious parents for their offspring, but instead with 'a crate of weird broken bits and cool smashed things'. More recently, as she has become aware of an underground movement of people who go on exploratory field trips to document abandoned sites (such as photographer Julia Sils), she prefers to leave objects in their original sites for all to appreciate.

As well as being a home, Paige's space is also a working studio that she offers to friends who would not otherwise have the space they need to create. 'That is the crux of the house here, it's a collective – sharing things and resources. Our lives are so much happier and richer when we can

She calls the loft the House of Collection, and virtually every inch of the space is covered in an eclectic assemblage of objects.

be part of a community.' Artist Sarah Sparkles spent three weeks there creating a motorcycle from crystals. 'It was more crystals than I had ever seen in my life.' Gonaway Ta Round is a regular visitor who uses an industrial sewing machine in the space to make costumes, clothes and decorations for hats. He also helps Paige repair her furniture, making elaborate patches for the arms of her mohair velvet couch with red leather and brass rivets.

Paige has also set up an area for her welding equipment and a performance area with an antique piano. She hires out the space for functions and performances and hosts annual Thanksgiving and Easter parties attended by a coterie of fascinating friends. While she dismisses the label of artist, which she feels implies a drive to create that she does not have, she believes that 'creativity is how you keep yourself energetically alive. The goal is to keep moving forward, to always learn new things, to always be involved in things.'

Certain aspects of Paige's childhood have been maintained and enshrined in her adult home life, while others have been rejected. Growing up, her ever-changing residential address was unsettling. 'I moved every year. I had a very chaotic, not very stable childhood so as a result; since I became an adult I haven't moved.' She has maintained the same residential address now for twenty-eight years, though with the gentrification of Williamsburg over the last few decades, she has had to fight hard to stay. When the building's owners tried to increase her rent, she and a few other tenants began a twelve-year court case that eventually led to the home being rent-stabilised. Now she can stay there, despite Williamsburg becoming one of the most desirable addresses in New York.

Having a stable home base has also freed her to spend time in communities of like-minded people outside New York. For ten years, she was a regular visitor to a Radical Faeries group located at the Short Mountain Sanctuary in Tennessee. The Radical Faerie movement was established in California in 1979 as a homosexual activist and anti-conformist group. Gonaway Ta Round, who is a regular of the group, describes it as 'a nexus for queer counter culture' and the Short Mountain Sanctuary as 'a place for creativity, for connecting with nature, for doing ritual work and healing from the patriarchy'. For Paige, it was like finding a family. 'This is how I grew up – the Cockettes, being on a goat farm, and then the drag culture. This was totally home for me.' While she is no longer a regular visitor, the Short Mountain Sanctuary experience reminded her of aspects of her upbringing that she loved and wanted to resurrect in her own home.

The House of Collection has allowed her to create her own eclectic chosen family, and gives her a space to forever call home. ◆

A NOTE ON IMAGES

All artwork is by the artist featured in the chapter, unless otherwise specified.

REBECCA REBOUCHÉ

10. Portrait of Rebecca wearing *Woodland Headdress* (2015), which she made for the Mardi Gras carnival in New Orleans.

15. Writing desk and pin board in her warehouse studio, New Orleans.

16. *Staccato* (2013), acrylic on canvas.

17. White grand piano sitting in the forest near Rebecca's treehouse, Louisiana.

18. Dresses hanging in the loft bedroom of the treehouse.

19. Rebecca holding one of her family patchwork quilts.

20. Sitting room in the loft. On wall: *You Think You're Sailing* (2014), acrylic on canvas, and *Gather Round* (2011), embroidery and fabric.

21. Series of plates and platters Rebecca created for Anthropologie.

22–23. Rebecca hugging one of the magnificent trees at Fontainebleau State Park, Louisiana.

BARNABA FORNASETTI

Artwork in this chapter is by Piero Fornasetti, unless otherwise specified.

24. Detail of a tray design, *Mano* (*Hand*), reinvented by Barnaba Fornasetti.

29. Library featuring: *Riga e Squadra* (*Ruler and Square*) desk, designed by Barnaba Fornasetti; Fornasetti waste paper basket *Strumenti da Disegno* (*Drawing Instruments*); Fornasetti screen *Battaglia Nave* (1954); and a 1960s Fornasetti crouching porcelain cat on the desk, Siamese, from the *Gatti Accovaciati* (*Curled Up Cats*) collection, created in the 1950s and 1960s.

30. Music room: red piano; Piero Fornasetti's drawing and work tools displayed on wall.

31. Red room, a guest bedroom, where all the books have red covers and include the word 'red' in their titles. Also featured: 19th-century walnut bed from Piedmont; 1950s Fornasetti bedside cabinet *Sole* (*Sun*) printed and lacquered by hand; 1950s Fornasetti red lacquered wooden lamp; Fornasetti vintage mirror *Specchio Magico* (*Magic Mirror*); Fornasetti cushion on the bed.

32. Barnaba in the music room with: Fornasetti mirror, *Grand Coromandel*; curtains made with Fornasetti fabric; Fornasetti vintage cube, *Geometrico* (*Geometric*) used as a side table.

33. Detail of the original drawing *Scoiattoli* (*Squirrels*) for a vintage Fornasetti tray.

34–35. Living room. Many of the mirrors, and the fireplace, were designed by Fornasetti. The room also features a white chesterfield artisan sofa, made for Piero Fornasetti in the 1960s, and a Fornasetti black-and-white storage bench *Piazza con Obelisco* (*Square with Obelisk*).

36. Previously Piero and Giulia's bedroom, this room is now a guest bedroom and features an early 20th-century cast-iron bedstead in gilt bronze.

37. The original drawing *Cappelli* (*Hats*) for Fornasetti umbrella stand, first produced in the 1950s.

38. Guest bedroom: Fornasetti wallpaper *Nuvole* (*Clouds*), by Cole & Son; 1950s Fornasetti curved chest of drawers, *Architettura*; 1950s Chiavarina chair originally designed by Giuseppe Gaetano Descalzi and produced by Fratelli Levaggi; 18th-century Italian oval wood mirror.

39. Piero Fornasetti's collection of Biedermeier glasses in Bohemia Crystal.

MILLE & UNE

40. Antique wooden table, with chandelier underskirt, displaying two of Claire Guiral's handmade crowns.

44–45. Claire's studio in Bordeaux.

46. Handmade paper dresses in Claire's studio.

47. Claire working on a paper dress in her studio.

48. An armchair in Claire's home, draped with her handmade necklaces.

49. Claire's kitchen with a cardboard crocodile wearing one of her handmade crowns and a necklace.

50–51. Ballroom installation of handmade paper dresses and accessories by Claire and curated by Valerie Mille as part of their collaboration 'Mille & Une'.

52. Papier-mâché balls on the floor in the parlour of the museum.

53. Matt gold silk curtains in the museum falling like a ball gown on the parquetry floor.

54–55. Entrance vestibule, decorated in gold leaf by Philippe Breton, who worked with Valerie on the museum's design.

57. Valerie, wearing one of Claire's handmade crowns and floor-length black lace dress.

58. Collection of Claire's handmade crowns.

J MORGAN PUETT

58. J Morgan Puett's home on her property, Mildred's Lane, Northeastern Pennsylvania.

63. Stand of young white pines at the crest of Mildred's Lane.

64. Chair and lace curtain inside the original c. 1830 farm house, Mildred House, located on Mildred's Lane.

65. Clockwise from top left: detail Mark Dion, Tate Thames Dig, Thames River Bankside, 1999; collection of Kansas artefacts from Grey Rabbit Puett's paleontological dig, 2007; examples from Morgan's collection of toy boats and models; cut nails from a collection of hardwares.

66. Two installations from ongoing Mildred Archaeology project. Part of an exhibition titled Mildred/Lillie Archaeology, installed in 2017 by fellows at The Mildred Complex(ity) Project Space in Narrowsburg, New York.

67. Morgan, in her handmade clothes, appearing from the door of *The Grafter's Shack* (2002), an installation built on the property in collaboration with visiting artists.

68–69. Kitchen inside main house.

70. Visiting artists Marek, Kristyna and Jakub Milde enjoy a pre-dinner drink on the verandah of main house.

71. Bedroom inside main house.

72–73. One of several dining areas inside main house. Photographs by Jeffrey Jenkins are mounted on the wall – part of a series titled *The Labor Portraits of Mildred's Lane* (2017), created in collaboration with Paul Bartow, Gary Graham, Cameron Klavsen, J Morgan Puett and David Wood. Art direction and styling of *The Labor Portraits of Mildred's Lane* by Rebecca Purcell.

FRANCESCO CLEMENTE

74. *Victory* (2015–2016), mixed media on canvas, propped on Frank Lloyd Wright chair in Francesco's studio.

79. Interior, living and dining room, Francesco and Alba's home. Features include: Frank Lloyd Wright dining table;

Ettore Sottsass chairs; West African mid-20th-century Senufo sculpture; Ettore Sottsass glass vases (on windowsill); Joseph Beuys drawing; Michele De Lucchi table lamp and Ettore Sottsass 1988 Mobile Giallo lacquered oak chest of drawers with gold leaf handles.

80. *Self Portrait in Disguise* (2011), oil on canvas.

81. Interior, living and dining room, showing Slit Gong wood statue from Vanuatu and Ettore Sottsass circular mirror.

82. Selection of limited edition pocket-sized books published by Hanuman Books.

83. Paint in jars inside Francesco's NoHo studio, New York.

84. Photograph of Indian ascetic Ramana Maharshi.

85. Kitchen view with three vases and detail of *In meiner Heimat XII* (2009), mixed media on paper.

86–87. Studio view with: Frank Lloyd Wright furniture; Ettore Sottsass side table; Jean Prouvé table; Fernwood Spirit Statue from Vanuatu; portrait of Rene Richard by Francesco (on right wall).

88–89. Collection of palette knives in Francesco's NoHo studio.

90. *Silver and Stone* (2003), watercolour on paper.

91. Portrait of Francesco.

JOSHUA YELDHAM

92. *Collection of Prayer Boxes* (2018).

97. View from the balcony at Joshua and Jo's home.

98. Portrait of Joshua.

99. *Silver Owl V* (2017), hand-carved aluminium with cane.

100. *Brothers* (2017), acrylic and cane on hand-carved board.

101. Jo and Indigo.

102. Jo's desk with Astier de Villatte swallow plate, ceramic gifts made by a friend, and personal notebooks.

103. Detail, *The Archer's Bow* (2017), acrylic and cane on hand-carved board.

104–105. Joshua looking on as Jude practises archery in front of Joshua's studio.

JEFFREY JENKINS

106. Collection of miniature animal trophy heads in wood and plastic.

111. Top: Random collection of textures, ephemera and objects surrounding a damaged then repaired wind-up animal, the first member of Jeffrey's *Misfit* collection (1975). Bottom: Early rubber farm animal repaired with tape and distorted by time.

112. Backyard with timber shack, soon to be a guest cottage.

113. *Untitled* (2015), cardboard and #4 granite gravel (study for a sculpture series based on childhood rock collection sets).

114–115. Workspace upstairs, which Jeffrey shares with his partner Rebecca.

116. Jeffrey on the front porch of the house.

117. Guest room wall covered in thrift-store animal tapestries and paintings, many created with 'paint-by-numbers' sets.

118. Jeffrey's vast collection of brushes in various shapes and designs.

119. View of a corner of the combined dining and living room.

ROBERT BAINES

120. Collection of silversmithing and jewellery hammers, and wood-and-hide mallets, from Robert's studio.

125. Robert and his dog Rufus walking up the path from the studio.

126. Robert's drawing studio including a shelf displaying his father's plaster slip cast moulds from c. 1943, when he worked at Fowler's pottery factory. Clipped to a board is a theoretical drawing by Robert.

127. Work in progress – spheres and hemispheres constructed by Robert in sterling silver wire.

128. Classic Australian corrugated-iron shed, c. 1920s, with loquat tree in the foreground, now a greenhouse and potting shed.

129. Assortment of crucibles used by Robert for melting gold and silver alloys.

130. Assorted goldsmithing steel punches for stamping, embossing, chasing and repoussé.

131. Wooden shipping box used to freight Robert's creations to museums and galleries around the world.

132. View of the main house.

133. Native Australian gum trees framing Robert's property.

ANNABELLE ADIE

134. *Links* (2013), ceramic and rope, shown installed on a wall with a painted form by Annabelle in matching acid yellow. The links can be installed in various ways forming a variety of shapes.

139. Armchair and ceramics in the studio with Annabelle's white glazed ceramic oval wall niche.

140–141. Living room with chairs and sofa draped with a giant linen Scottish flag and Union Jack created by Annabelle.

142. Clockwise from top left: Hand-painted linen swatches; one of Annabelle's white glazed-ceramic wall niches displaying *Where Are We Heading?* by Sumner Wells (H. Hamilton, 1947); detail, *Key Hole* (2008), ceramic and white plaster; a collection of Annabelle's ceramic and painting works including *Key Hole* (2008), ceramic and white plaster; *Sculpted Chain and Rope* (2013), white glazed ceramic and hiking rope, and *Extra Parts* (2013), ceramic and rope, and *Untitled* (2005), paint pigment with an acrylic base on wood board. In the same image, displayed on sidetable: Annabelle Adie, *Sculpted Ceramic Chain* (2014), ceramic.

143. Clockwise from top left: Work coats for painting hanging in the studio; main bedroom; paint brushes from the studio; *Test Tubes with Acid Yellow Cord* (2016), ceramic and rope, *Three Balls and Label with Fluorescent Orange Hiking Rope* (2015), ceramic and rope, *Untitled* (2005), pigment on wood, *Needing Space* (2005), pigment on wood.

144. Wooden frame, inspired by an old Italian kitchen wall frame for pans, allowing for a mix of inspiring objects and personal pieces.

145. Wall painting, *Growth* (2009), created by Annabelle, in pencil and gesso, displayed above the white marble mantelpiece. Also displayed: *Separate Parts* (2016), gesso and oil on wood panel; more creations in fabric, paper and ceramic.

146. Homemade paint swatches propped on *One of Those Breakthrough Days* (2014), oil on canvas.

147. Portrait of Annabelle wearing the family tartan

148–149. *Drops* (2009), white glazed ceramic, framed on wall by Annabelle's painted shapes.

NATHALIE LÉTÉ

150. Studio sitting area with giant papier-mâché rabbit for Nathalie's 2015 solo exhibition at La Piscine museum in Roubaix. Paintings on various themes created from 2000–2018. The couch features Villa des Roses fabric and the armchair is covered in Bébés Animaux fabric – both fabrics she designed for Thevenon. Nathalie designed the cushions for Room Seven, Po-Paris and Monoprix. Plates and tins also for Monoprix.

154. Nathalie standing under an umbrella of her own design outside her Ivry-sur-Seine studio.

155. Ceramic flowers by Nathalie displayed on her *Mushroom Forest* wallpaper, commissioned by Anthopologie.

156–157. Nathalie's showroom. She worked with architect Nicolas André and carpenters and wood sculptors Antonis Cardew and Clément Poma to create furniture for the space. The space features Nathalie's silk scarves, pendant light fittings, woven rugs and baskets in collaboration with Po-Paris, and printed tables made in collaboration with Bazartherapy.

158. Detail, *Les Chiens Fô* (2017), acrylic on paper.

159. Detail of embroidered cat cushion designed by Nathalie, and Jungle Tray created by the artist for Avenida Home.

160–161. Cabinet in Nathalie's studio displaying some of her vast toy collection.

GAVIN BROWN AND PETER CURNOW

162. Gavin (left) and Peter (right) on the landing separating their apartments.

167. Entrance hall in Peter's apartment, looking through to the landing. On the right of the doorway is a wooden panel by English artist Jason Harcup. The burgundy-and-gold wallpaper was printed by Peter using two 18th-century cherrywood printing blocks belonging to Gavin. Peter used the same blocks to print the outer fabric of the oversized lampshade, which was made for Fringe Furniture in collaboration with Melbourne artist Sara Thorn. On the far right of the frame is an Oceanic tribal mask. The indoor plant sits on a stick wood stool, from Martin Allan Antiques. The settee is from a suite of Moroccan furniture, which Gavin inherited from his friend David 'Pussy' Aboud.

168–169. Dining room in Peter's apartment. Centred above the fireplace on the far wall is a mansard window frame, now used as a mirror, flanked by two oxidised lanterns and six Fornasetti plates. On the left wall is a large work by Chris Orr, *Fang Shui* (2015), pigment print on archival rag paper. A lacquered console from Kyoto displays treasures including a glass sculpture by Mark Douglass, a white Rosenthal vase and a hand-carved wooden figure wearing a Navajo coral necklace.

170. Sitting area in Peter's apartment viewed through Chinese lacquer door panels. On far wall: Gavin Brown, *Wildflowers with Figure* (2013), oil on canvas.

171. Wooden infant Christ figure adorned with amber beads and coral earrings.

172–173. Gavin working in his St Kilda studio. Right of window: Gavin Brown, *Bees and Butterflies* (2015), printing ink and oil on canvas.

174–175. Gavin's sitting room with red lacquer Chinese cabinet displaying gilded Italian and Portuguese candle sticks and a wooden Quan Yin carving; early 19th-century French chair; cushions made by Peter from 18th-century Turkish tapestry fragments; orange velvet-covered Regency style stool and a circular Vietnamese wedding dowry box (in foreground); paisley frieze (above the picture rail) hand printed by Gavin from his Lino cut printing blocks.

REBECCA PURCELL

176. View of the sitting room showing a painting from an antique shop in South Carolina, purchased for its androgynous quality and peculiar composition. Objects on the console include: collection of geometric shapes Rebecca created from sewn cardboard pieces covered in magazine paper or velvet; collection of velvet-covered jewellery boxes.

181. Objects Rebecca has collected and created for styling assemblages, including ovals covered in worn velvet, saved vintage fabric or paper scraps.

182. Collection of coin purses.

183. Shelf in Rebecca's kitchen.

184–185. Living room.

186. Objects from Rebecca's many collections, including amulets and talismans, hat pins and shapes covered in vintage fabric.

187. Portrait of Rebecca.

SIMONE BENDIX AND HELENE SCHJERBECK

188. Paper cut collage with fresh spring flowers and birds.

192–193. Simone (right) and Helene (left) on the balcony of the Parisian apartment Simone shares with her husband Kasper Winding and their children.

194–195. Living room. Far left wall: photo of Simone by Kasper; centre: sofa with Simone's handmade cushions in fabrics purchased around Marché Saint Pierre in Montmartre; mantelpiece: papercut flowers in opaline vases and framed image by Rebecca Langebaek; back wall: works by Thomas Winding, (Kasper's father), Viktor IV (Walter Karl Glück), and an unknown artist; right of fireplace: small painting by Danish artist Lin Utzon, silver gelatin print by Marc Hom, *Louise Bourgeois with Arms Stretched* (1996).

196. Papercuts made from French music books; small leather lipstick case by Edition Poshette with leather cord and mirror inside.

197. One of the children's bedrooms.

198. Ceramic and wire flowers Simone inherited from her mother, reimagined as a decorative still life placed on a paper-lined jewellery box.

199. Simone (right) and Helene (left) working on papercuts. Pendant lamps by Tom Dixon, table top by Kasper (designed to look like a surf board), *Tulip Chairs* by Eero Saarinen, designed in 1955/56 for Knoll in New York.

GREG IRVINE

200. One of Greg's paintings-in-progress in his studio.

204. Collection of vintage and antique umbrellas and parasols.

205. Velvet cushions made from vintage fabrics on the couch in the sitting room.

206. Kitchen, showing shelves of treasures including a green glass collection, containers of bakelite flatware and vintage food tins.

207. Art Nouveau chair with elephant fabric insert painted by Greg. On shelf above, French enamelware jugs and serving bowl.

208–209. Sitting room. Features include: rare Edwardian oriental dresser with lacquer panels; tortoise-shell bamboo chair; antique wicker furniture; collection of antique porcelain plates including Dutch colonial pieces from Indonesia and Chinese blue-and-white bowls, plates and platters.

210. Greg in his studio.

211. Statue of 1920s film star Theda Bara, forming a lamp base. Portrait of Greg Irvine by Australian artist Lewis Miller.

212. Bathroom with original 19th-century claw-foot bath and pressed-tin ceilings, accessorised by French enamel jugs, early Victorian leather boots, and vintage combs and brushes.

213. Vintage figurines populating a work table in Greg's studio.

SARAH DE TELIGA

214. *Fragments from the Louvre* (2012–2017), oil on tin can lids.

219. Artwork on bedroom wall. From top: George Tjungurrayi, date and title unknown, acrylic on canvas; Tim Johnson, title unknown, but subject of the painting is a portrait of Aboriginal artist (c. 1985), oil on canvas; Nancy Carnegie Tjakura, date unknown, oil on canvas (Kayili Artists exhibition 2007, William Mora Galleries); Sarah de Teliga, *Metro* (2007), oil on board; Sarah de Teliga, *Floating* (2016), oil on board; Tim Johnson, title unknown, 1989, oil on canvas; bottom left Anatjari Tjakamarra, Portrait of John Jagamara, date and title unknown; bottom right: Sarah de Teliga, *Tour de Montparnasse, Paris* (2014), oil on board. Quilt on bed handmade by Rae de Teliga, Sarah's mother, in 2009.

220. Sitting room. From left to right, starting top left: George Jawaranga Wurramara, date and title unknown, earth pigment on bark; Margaret Bevan, *The Brolgas in the Moonlight* (c. 1960), oil on board; Sarah de Teglia, *Cevennes* (2010), oil on wooden board; Sarah de Teglia, *Yoke Planet* (2016), oil on board; Sarah de Teglia, *Rubbish Bin Portrait* (2017), oil on board; Sarah de Teglia, *Medici Planet* (2001 and 2016), oil on board; Barpua, *Stingray* (c. 1965), natural earth pigments on eucalyptus bark; Michael Snape, *Star* (2001), steel; Sarah de Teliga, *Wedding Anniversary Blossom and Snow* (2016), oil on board; Sarah de Teliga, *Family* (2016), oil on board. Three shimmering rock sculptures mounted on right by Martin McNulty. Sofa: Svenskt Tenn, fabric: Joseph Frank.

221. *Snowballs* (2004), oil on wood.

222. *Perizonium* (2012–2014), oil on wooden panel.

223. Portrait of Sarah.

224. Masking spheres Sarah uses to block areas of paint when working on the surrounding space.

225. Sitting area in bedroom. On wall from top: Margaret Bevan, *Pelicans in Flood, Coorong South Australia* (c. 1970), oil on wood; Sarah de Teliga, *The Ambush of Miss Kitty* (2018), wood and plastic; Sarah de Teliga, *Rooftops and Eiffel Tower* (2014), oil and phosphorus paint on wood panel; Sarah de Teliga, *Rockpools Balmoral* (2014), oil on wood panel. Chair by Joseph Frank, 1930. Rug by Gunnar Asplund, 1930. The photo on the desk is of Linus, one of Sarah and Robert's two sons by Jeremy Stigter (c. 2006).

BELLA MEYER

226. Detail of flowers from Fleurs Bella, Bella's flower studio in New York.

231. Bella working at the desk that once belonged to her grandfather Marc Chagall.

232. Flower detail taken at Fleurs Bella.

233. Staff creating flower bouquets at Fleurs Bella.

234–235. Combined sitting room, library and office, inside Bella's apartment in New York.

GIOVANNA CARBONI

236. *Tiamo* scratched into the wall of the home office Giovanna shares with her husband, Sergio Carnevale.

240. Python in bottle of formaldehyde on the shelf of an antique cabinet that Giovanna restored and repurposed.

241. Portrait of Giovanna.

242. Clockwise from top left: Fornasetti key made from cardboard; dining chair and table restored by Giovanna; collection of family portraits; dried leaves in a woven basket.

243. Giovanna's office desk with framed anatomical drawings on the wall.

244–245. Sitting room inside Giovanna's apartment.

LUKE SCIBERRAS

246. View of the façade of Luke's home, an 1873 Georgian cottage.

251. Kitchen featuring works by Luke Sciberras, John Olsen, Garry Shead and Janet Dawson.

252–253. Luke in his studio.

254. Pots of paintbrushes in the studio.

255. Easel and floor detail in the studio.

256–257. Kitchen. Artworks on far wall by Elisabeth Cummings, Ben Quilty, Billy Benn, Donald Friend, Jedda-Daisy Culley, Tony Tuckson, Euan Macleod, Jumaadi, Johnny Young, Reg Mombassa and Luke Sciberras.

258. Detail of door to guest house.

259. Black and white gum trees on the road to Hill End.

MARCO AROSIO

260. Exterior view of Villa Singer, Marco's home in Milan.

265. View looking through to the light-filled sun room.

266. Powder room: purple cane chair and Liberty wallpaper designed by William Morris and printed in the late 1960s.

267. Sitting room with works of art by Marco's friends including Aldo Mondino, Luigi Ontani, Massimo Kaufmann, Luigi Serafini and Letizia Cariello.

268. Sitting room with marble fireplace and collected treasures.

269. Chinese style servomuto painted by Raja Schwahn-Reichmann; lightbox by Andrea Mastrovito; paintings by Eugene Berman and Fabrizio Clerici.

PAIGE STEVENSON

270. Detail in living room with handmade and salvaged objects, artefacts and furniture. Gonaway Ta Round repaired the arms of the mohair couch using red leather and brass rivets.

275. One of over sixty indoor plants in Paige's loft.

276–277. Kitchen featuring relics rescued from abandoned buildings in New York, Pennsylvania and Connecticut.

278. Guest bedroom.

279. Paige sitting among her indoor plants, wearing dress and hat made by Gonaway Ta Round.

280–281. Sitting area: mohair velvet couch; collections of salvaged treasures mounted on wall.

ACKNOWLEDGEMENTS

This book has taken me on a creative adventure around the world, and along the way I have been encouraged, supported and guided by many people.

Firstly, I would like to gratefully acknowledge and thank all those featured in this book, as well as their partners and families, who opened their private homes and studios to me. I have learned important things from all of you, and been moved by the beauty you bring to the world. I am deeply thankful for the trust you have shown me.

Marina Cukeric and Andy Quin helped with the production of the photo shoots and injected the process with loads of fun. My parents, Richard and Lynette Lea, generously discussed all the stories and adventures in the book and provided important guidance and suggestions along the way on the text and images.

Thank you also to those people who suggested possible subjects for this project: Lou Phillips, Felicity Rulikowski, Penelope Scott, Simone Bendix, Christine Taylor Patten, Julia Lea, Barnaba Fornasetti and Yuki Tintori. Friends who have encouraged and supported me while doing this project: Caroline Cox, Sabina Reid, Rebecca Ascher, Amanda Cole, Nikki Ansell, Anne-Marie Kearns, Abby Cox, Vickie Tabain, Jane Webster, Sally Balharrie, Nicola Lester, Garth Davis, Sophie Griffiths, Max Walker, Bradley Seymour, Nathalie Kemp, Bec Cole, Lara Dowd, Josephine Corcoran and Nicola Granter. Scott Livesey for your thoughtful insights into contemporary Australian art. And Penelope Scott for your wonderful friendship and support, and your unwavering and thoughtful interest in all the details of this project.

To my husband, Tim Hunt, and our children, Issy and Freddie, thank you for all the love and support you have given me during this project, and for the breakfast and dinnertime chats about the stories and people in the book.

Special thanks to Kirsten Abbott from Thames & Hudson. When you approached me to discuss this idea at the end of 2016, I was thrilled, and I am grateful for the opportunity to work together on this book. I have appreciated your input and vision for the project, your guidance, words of wisdom and encouragement along the way. Heartfelt thanks also to the wonderful team at Thames & Hudson and to graphic designer Daniel New for his beautiful work.

Front cover: Fornasetti invitation card,
photographed in Giovanna Carboni's home in Milan.

1. Detail, illustration *Braccio Ingioiellato* (*Jewelled Arm*)
by Piero Fornasetti, 1950s.

2. Detail, paint palette in Gavin Brown's studio.

4. Detail, pinboard in Barnaba Fornasetti's home
in Milan with Fornasetti illustrations, magazine
clippings and collected mementos.

6. Cabinet inside Barnaba Fornasetti's home in Milan.

296. Handmade dress by Claire Guiral hanging
on the back of a door inside her home in Bordeaux.

Back cover: Bedroom in Casa Fornasetti, Milan.
Previously Piero Fornasetti and Giulia Gelmi's
bedroom, this room is now a guest bedroom and
features an early 20th-century cast-iron bedstead
in gilt bronze.

First published in Australia in 2018
by Thames & Hudson Australia Pty Ltd
11 Central Boulevard Portside Business Park
Port Melbourne Victoria 3207
ABN: 72 004 751 964

www.thamesandhudson.com.au

21 20 19 18   5 4 3 2 1

ISBN: 978 1 76076000 9 0

A catalogue record for this
book is available from the
National Library of Australia

NATIONAL
LIBRARY
OF AUSTRALIA

Design: Daniel New
Editing: Lorna Hendry
Printed and bound in China by C&C